OVERCOMING ADVERSITY THROUGH MIRACLES

DEACON STEVE GRECO

Copyright © 2018 Deacon Steve Greco

All rights reserved.

**ISBN-13:
978-1987595772**

**ISBN-10:
1987595777**

DEDICATION

It is impossible to go through life without major adversity hitting us right between the eyes. It is not if but when. The question is how will we handle it? The answer, I feel, is a combination of your faith in God and the support system you have in your life.

I am very blessed to have a tremendous support group of people who love me starting with my wife Mary Anne, my children, my Spirit Filled Hearts family and my many friends. It is to those who stand with me and my Lord and Savior Jesus Christ that I dedicate this book.

ACKNOWLEDGMENTS

Scripture texts in this work are taken from the *New American Bible, revised edition* © 2010, 1991, 1986, 1970 Confraternity of Christian Doctrine, Washington, D.C. and are used by permission of the copyright owner. All Rights Reserved. No part of the New American Bible may be reproduced in any form without permission in writing from the copyright owner.

I want to thank all those who helped me make this book a reality. Katie Hughes who inspires me with her great faith, Geoff Gudelman who created the cover and the many people helping me with prayers and support. Andrew Laubacher whose work gives me hope for the future, thank you for your introduction. Ray Joske for his inspiration and work on the ***Miracle Index.***™

I also want to thank Cindy Brauer, my editor, for her wonderful work and dedication on the book.

FOREWARD

Our world is in need of light. As the darkness begins to become more evident in our culture the need for the light of Christ is more urgent than ever. The Church must awaken to the reality that we have Christ in us, the hope of glory, this is good news. Deacon Steve Greco lays out the truth that through Christ nothing is impossible and if we want to be the light of the world, we need to know who we are and why we exist on this planet.

We were made to live and act in the supernatural love of God everywhere we go. Not just at Mass or when we pray the rosary, but in everyday normal situations. We can be light in every place that is dark, the light will always win. This book, I believe, is the answer to hungry heart of every human person, a supernatural encounter with the Trinity. God wants to partner with us to bring the kingdom everywhere we go. Deacon Steve brings this clear reality that we were made to be saints and we can walk in the power of the Holy Spirit even today. This precise exhortation given in this book will make scripture and stories come alive and demonstrate the goodness of God and that he still acts today.

Throughout history, the saints demonstrate what is possible when we believe the words Jesus said, "You will do the same works that I did and even greater"(John 14:12). If the Church began to understand that miracles are a part of the normal Christian life today what would Sunday Mass look like? I know it wouldn't be empty and just a lot of old people, but it would be full because people today are looking for God and if we just exercised the gifts God has given each person it would impact the world. This is all to be done in love; the miracles are meant to demonstrate the reality that the kingdom is here, not to point to ourselves. Yet, this renewal of the supernatural must become normal. It's false humility to think that you shouldn't pray for the supernatural; Jesus said you would do it. Do you believe God in the flesh?

Evangelization today will not be effective unless we operate in love with and through the gifts and fruits of the Holy Spirit. Everything about the Christian faith is supernatural. You believe in prayer, the resurrection, virgin birth, saints, angels, Eucharist? These are all "unnatural" things, so why don't we believe God can work miracles through us? We're sinners; we get it. Let's start talking about how we are sons and daughters and remember the fact that Jesus chose 12 messed-up dudes to change the world. He can definitely use any average person like myself.

My prayer is that this book would bring you into the reality of your inheritance and your purpose is life, which is simple. To make disciples of all nations. And what is the best way to do that? Well, Jesus is the model, and he sure didn't just talk about God. Our programs, fish-fry's, pastoral councils, worship groups and bingo nights aren't going to impact others if they don't bring in the power of the gospel. Look at the lives of the apostles and the saints of the Church; they walked in power and love. If you think God can't you use you, think again; you're never too far away. This book will bring you great joy. Pope Francis says we need to stop looking like we just got out of a funeral all the time. If God is real and we have been saved from sin and the punishment of sin, the joy of the Savior should flow into every part of life, even on bad days.

Deacon Steve is on fire and really believes in the power of the Holy Spirit and that we can heal the sick, raise the dead, cleanse lepers and cast out demons, as every Catholic should.

Jesus said we could do it. His ability to make the scriptures come alive will help you overcome any obstacle in your life. This book is anointed and will bring the reader into their destiny. Everyone is looking to answers to big questions; we don't claim to have all the answers, but we do know who does. When we turn to Jesus and repent, he comes running to us with the Father and Spirit to make us new again. May this reading bring newness and power to your life. I hope you realize you can do the works of Jesus and the best way to preach the gospel is not in talk but in power! Come Holy Spirit!

Andrew Laubacher

CONTENTS

Introduction

1	The Miracle Index	9
2	Why Me?	16
3	Conquering Fear	19
4	Receiving God's Love	23
5	Baptism of the Holy Spirit	31
6	Expectant Faith	43
7	Winning the Battlefield of the Mind	49
8	Living the Mercy of Christ	57
9	Living a Life of Hope	66
10	Healing of Memories	72
11	Living the Joy of Christ	78

12	Expect and Experience Miracles	86
13	Transformation through Praise	92
14	The Power of Living a Sacramental Life	102
15	Called to Evangelize	107
16	Becoming the Light of the World	113
17	Answering the Call	121
18	Called to be Holy	127

OVERCOMING ADVERSITY THROUGH MIRACLES

INTRODUCTION

Jesus loves us! Passionately! Totally! Completely!

If that is the case, why don't we feel it? Why are there so many problems and challenges, so much suffering?

Jesus was very clear that we would face challenges and troubles in our lives.

> John 16:33 "In the world you will have trouble, take courage, I have conquered the world."

It is not if, but when, we will encounter adversity. What do we do when adversity strikes? Do we turn to the flesh and the world's promises? Do we fear? Do we become depressed? Do we retreat from God?

Jesus told us to come to him when we are labored and burdened.

> Matthew 11:28-30 "Come to me, all you who labor and are burdened, and I will give you rest. Take my yoke upon you and learn from me, for I am meek and humble of heart and you will find rest for yourselves. For my yoke is easy and my burden is light."

With Jesus at our side and in our heart, through his grace, we can conquer any challenge and adversity that come upon us.

> 1 Corinthians 10:13 "No trial has come to you but what is human. God is faithful and will not let you be tried beyond your strength; but with the trial he will also provide a way out, so that you may be able to bear it."

So many times we want Jesus to be like a gift-giving Santa Claus, while we, in turn, give back very little. Jesus wants <u>all</u> of us. Total surrender. He wants a personal relationship with each of us. We must encounter the *Risen Christ* and be completely transformed through his love and forgiveness. We must deny ourselves, our flesh, our selfish desires and the world's impulses and take up our cross.

> Matthew 16:24-26 "Then Jesus said to his disciples, 'Whoever wishes to come after me, must deny himself, take up his cross, and follow me. For whoever wishes to save his life will lose it, but whoever loses his life for my sake will find it. What profit would there be for one to gain the whole world and forfeit his life? Or what can one give in exchange for his life?'"

Some may question the title of this book, *Overcoming Adversity Through Miracles*. How do the words "miracles" and "adversity" go together? The *Catholic Encyclopedia* definition of miracle is "wonders performed by supernatural power as signs of some special mission or gift and explicitly ascribed to God."

When I give my talk, "Expect and Experience Miracles," I offer audience members this specific

OVERCOMING ADVERSITY THROUGH MIRACLES

definition of a miracle. Then I ask the them, "Do you believe in miracles?" and "Have you experienced a miracle in your life?" Consistently, over 90 percent of the people raise their hands.

What about you? Do you believe in God's miracles? Do you believe all things are possible through him? Do you believe Jesus' words in John's gospel?

> John 14:12 "Amen, Amen, I say to you, whoever believes in me will do the works that I do, and will do greater ones than these, because I am going to the Father."

Our ability to believe in God's ongoing supernatural intervention in our lives is a huge part of our transformation to become more like Christ. Jesus gave me the insight that many do not believe in either his love for them or that he wants to bless their lives. It is for this reason I created the *Miracle Index*™ and wrote this book.

This book is intended to offer hope, increase faith and inspire courage when we face trials and to impart encouragement in the midst of trials. In these pages, I provide tools to help you grow spiritually and receive the joy and abundant life that God desires for you.

DEACON STEVE GRECO

OVERCOMING ADVERSITY THROUGH MIRACLES

MIRACLE INDEX™

God uses miracles routinely in our lives to shower his love upon us, please take a moment to reflect and understand how prepared you are to experience miracles in your life by determining your *Miracle Index* before you begin this book and again when you complete it.

Just answer each of these 10 questions on a scale of 1 to 10; **where 1 is low or no faith and 10 is a high degree of faith**. Note your score so you can determine your index after you read this book. **Are you prepared to experience miracles?**

1. How would you describe the depth of your faith in comparison to the "faith to move mountains?"
2. Do you expect miracles in your life?
3. Have you totally surrendered every aspect of your life to Christ?
4. Do you pray daily for miracles to occur?
5. Do you struggle with forgiveness of others, especially those closest to you?
6. Do you understand the distinct types of miracles that can occur?
7. Are you comfortable with determining if something in your life can be called a miracle?
8. Do you have the gift of perseverance in both your prayer life and your faith?
9. Do you share with others the miracles that God has provided you?
10. Are you thankful for the miracles in your life?

CHAPTER 1

THE MIRACLE INDEX

To understand miracles is to understand the faith of the Centurion as recorded in Matthew's gospel.

> Matthew 8:6-8 "'Lord, my servant is lying at home paralyzed, suffering dreadfully' He said to him, 'I will come and cure him.' The centurion said in reply, 'Lord, I am not worthy to have you enter under my roof; only say the word and my servant will be healed.'"

Why did Jesus get so excited about the faith of the Centurion? Why did he say in a subsequent passage:

> Matthew 8:10 "Amen, I say to you, in no one in Israel, have I found such faith."

OVERCOMING ADVERSITY THROUGH MIRACLES

Jesus tries to teach us that through faith we can move mountains of adversity.

> Mark 11:22-23 "'Have faith in God. Amen, I say to you, whoever says to this mountain, "Be lifted up to the sea," and does not doubt in his heart but believes what he says will happen, it shall be done for him.'"

For this reason, the very first question in the *Miracle Index*™ is:

1. How would you describe the depth of your faith in comparison to the "faith that moves mountains?"

After 40 years in the healing ministry, I have found that having faith in God to act makes a profound difference in our ability to experience miracles.

Matthew 7:7 "Ask and it will be given to you; seek and you will find; knock and the door will be opened to you."

2. Do you expect miracles in your life?

It is critical to expect and experience miracles!

I have found it interesting that some people become very uncomfortable when I suggest they ask for miracles. Why? Did not Jesus tell us to ask anything in his name? Ask and we will receive? I believe that the desire for miracles brings us closer to Jesus and better able build up his church—and that is what God wants for us. Jesus clearly instructed us to ask him for anything according to his will.

> 1 John 5:14 "And we have this confidence in him, that if we ask anything according to his will, he hears us."

Remember, a miracle is God's special grace and power. We have not been left orphans, but rather, we have the power and authority in the name of Jesus when we operate in his will.

> 1 Corinthians 4:20 "For the kingdom of God is not a matter of talk but power."

3. Have you totally surrendered every aspect of your life to Christ?

OVERCOMING ADVERSITY THROUGH MIRACLES

A critical element of the *Miracle Index*™ is we must surrender without compromise to the love of Jesus. Most of the time, we hold back certain parts of our lives because we believe we know best. Was that not the sin of Adam and Eve in the garden? Thinking we know better than God what is good for us?

4. Do you pray daily for miracles to occur?

Jesus is our best friend. Do we not communicate frequently with our closest friends and family regarding what is important to us? God wants us to be intimate with him regarding our needs and striving for holiness. Pray throughout each day for God to intervene in your life.

5. Do you struggle with forgiveness of others, especially those closest to you?

I often remark that beside faith, the lack of forgiveness is one of the biggest obstacles to experiencing miracles in our lives.

> Mark 11:24-25 "Therefore I tell you, all that you ask for in prayer, believe that you will

receive it and it shall be yours. When you stand to pray, forgive anyone against whom you have a grievance, so that your heavenly Father can in turn forgive you your transgressions."

6. Do you understand the distinct types of miracles that can occur?

So many times we put God in a box. We limit what we believe he can accomplish in our lives. Perhaps we believe we only get one or two special favors before reaching our lifetime limit on God's miraculous gifts. Not so! God wants to grant us miracles in every conceivable way. He doesn't run out of miracles.

> Ephesians 1:3: "Blessed be the God and Father of our Lord Jesus Christ, who has blessed us in Christ with every spiritual blessing in the heavens."

7. Are you comfortable with determining if something in your life can be called a

miracle?

Often, we are confused and reluctant to call some occurrence or experience in our lives a miracle. I find it much more comfortable to identify miracles when I focus on God's supernatural power and intervention in my life. Based upon this recognition, assess how often God has blessed you by his power and authority.

8. Do you have the gift of perseverance in both your prayer life and your faith?

Perseverance is a foundation of holiness. We need endurance in "running the race." Perseverance and endurance will open the door to our hearts, minds and souls to receive what God wants to give us.

> Hebrews 10:36 "You need endurance to do the will of God and receive what he has promised."

9. Do you share with others the miracles God has provided you?

I strongly believe when we tell others about God's love and how he has worked miracles in our lives, our blessings will be enhanced.

10. Are you thankful for the miracles your life?

The final question in the *Miracle Index*™ concerns thanksgiving.

> 1 Thessalonians 5:18 "In all circumstances give thanks, for this is the will of God for you in Christ Jesus."

When we are thankful, I believe, God opens the floodgates of Heaven to pour out blessings for us.

CHAPTER 2

WHY ME?

Have you ever asked yourself this question, "Why me? I do so much for you Lord, and this is how I get repaid?"

Perhaps you have felt as Jesus did on the cross, "Why am I abandoned?"

> Psalm 22:2-3 "My God, my God, why have you abandoned me? / Why so far from my call for help, / from my cries of anguish? / My God, I call by day, but you do not answer; / by night, but I have no relief."

For me, one of the biggest trials in my life occurred when my daughter notified me she had lung cancer, a terminal disease in most cases. An even greater trial happened six weeks later when she called me from an East Coast-area hospital to tell me the cancer had entered her heart. She said that she might not last the night and was giving her final goodbye.

I remember crying out in anguish! "Why would you take my only daughter away from me? All I have done is try to follow you, devote my life to sharing your love, and this is how you reward me?"

A human response. Afterword, I felt the need to repent. To ask God for forgiveness for not trusting him. I then felt the Lord say to me deep in my soul, "I love your daughter, my daughter, more than you can ever imagine."

Suffering and trials are difficult for most of us. We cry out to God to fix things: our family, job, health, marriage, relationships, finances, etc. But we think we know best how our lives should run. We don't ask for God's will; rather, we usually ask God to do our will.

What is the purpose of adversity and suffering?

> 1 Peter 1:6-7 "In this you rejoice, although now for a little while you may have to suffer through various trials, so that the genuineness of your faith, more precious than gold that is perishable even though tested by fire, may prove to be for praise, glory, and honor at the revelation of Jesus Christ."

Our suffering does have a purpose! I often have felt achieving holiness is impossible without experiencing trials. We are well underway to achieving the crown of

OVERCOMING ADVERSITY THROUGH MIRACLES

life when we undergo trials.

> James 1:12 "Blessed is the man who perseveres in temptation, for when he has been proved he will receive the crown of life that he promised to those who love him."

Another significant result in undergoing suffering is learning how to grow closer to God.

> James 1: 2-4 "Consider it joy my brothers, when you encounter various trials. For you know that the testing of your faith produces perseverance and let perseverance be perfect, so that you may be perfect and complete, lacking in nothing."

Jesus told us that we must endure to be the end to be saved.

> Matthew 24:13 "But the one that perseveres to the end will be saved."

My brothers and sisters, life is hard. We know that. However, we have so much to look forward to. Forever in Heaven with Jesus!

CHAPTER 3

CONQUERING FEAR

When we undergo trials, we fight the battle of fear. Fear of the current situation, fear of the future, fear of what will happen to us, our loved ones, our family, marriage, relationships, job, children, friends and, well, you get the picture. At times, life seems overwhelming, even to those we perceive as holy.

We are not alone; nearly every saint has had doubts, fear and dark moments of despair. St. Mother Theresa, in letters written in confidence to her confessors, had times of doubt. She wrote about having no faith and about thoughts that gave her untold agony. She described putting on a cloak that covered her despair with a smile. Saint Therese of Lisieux described her fear as being in a night of nothingness.

Fear is crippling and immobilizing. Fear is our enemy. What conquers fear? God's love.

OVERCOMING ADVERSITY THROUGH MIRACLES

> 1 John 4:18 "There is no fear in love, but perfect love drives out fear because fear has to do with punishment, and so one who fears is not yet perfect in love."

When we are open to God's love, we are open to hope. Transformed by God's love, we trust in him. As in the Divine Mercy devotion, we say with confidence, "Jesus, I Trust In You, Jesus I Trust In You, Jesus, I Trust In You."

When we hope and trust, God's love showers on us the peace that passes all understanding. We do not tremble and fear.

> Romans 15:13 "May the .God of hope fill you with all joy and peace in believing, so that you may abound in hope by the power of the holy Spirit."

One of the most important scriptures for us to memorize and have rooted in our hearts and souls is found in Paul's letter to the Romans.

> Romans 8:28 "We know that all things work for good for those who love God, who are called according to his purpose."

Do we believe this scripture passage? Is this belief an important part of our lives? When we believe God is real and that he cares about us and loves us more than we can ever imagine, everything changes. Our doubts, fears and anxieties melt away.

I love to be with groups of believers and declare the phrase, "God is good!" Their response, "All the time!" echoes the scripture in Thessalonians.

> 1 Thessalonians 5:18 "In all circumstances give thanks, for this is the will of God for you in Christ Jesus."

In the midst of trials, it is difficult to understand or accept that God has a purpose for everything in our life. Many of us try to figure out his plan for us. We attempt to understand why things happen the way that they do. We even plan our lives according to our human understanding. "We plan, God laughs."

No! No! No! Please do not try to figure out every aspect of what happens to you or what may happen to you. We do not comprehend God's ways.

> Isaiah 55:9 "For as the heavens are higher than the earth, / so are my ways, / my thoughts higher than your thoughts."

We also see Jesus telling us not to worry or try to figure out our lives.

> Matthew 6:34 "Do not worry about tomorrow; tomorrow will take care of itself. Sufficient for a day is its own evil."

Focusing on God's goodness and love transforms us, leaving no room for fear in our lives! This is always true, but especially when we are in crisis.

OVERCOMING ADVERSITY THROUGH MIRACLES

A friend of mine was 7½ months pregnant. She began bleeding and went to her doctor. Her physician gave her news no person wants to hear. They could not hear the baby's heartbeat. She was told to go to the emergency room to have labor induced.

My friend had recently read the book I wrote, *Expect and Experience Miracles*, and took it out of her purse. Rather than fear, she asked God for more faith. The baby had been pronounced dead for 45 minutes when she was in the emergency room. Still, she believed!

Crying, she begged the physicians and nurses, "Will you check the heartbeat one more time?"

And sure enough, they found the heartbeat! Eighteen doctors were called in to certify the baby was alive since it had been legally pronounced dead! Six weeks later, she delivered a totally healthy baby boy. Ten pounds, one ounce!

A month after giving birth, my friend came to our prayer meeting with her healthy baby and beaming with joy! Amen!

No one can outdo God's love. Trust in him. Rebuke fear! You will see miracles in your life!

CHAPTER 4

RECEIVING GOD'S LOVE

Everything changes when we realize God loves us unconditionally! This realization is not easy for many of us. We may have grown up in an environment in which we were rewarded with love when we did what our parents wanted us to do.

I am a second-generation Italian American. Both sets of grandparents immigrated from southern Italy sometime around 1910 and were married soon after arriving in this country. My mother was born in 1917 and my father in 1913.

Both were products of the Depression. You had to earn everything you got. My father taught me "pride of ownership." If I worked hard and was successful, then I was a good person. When were successful in life, the family would love me and give me a lot of recognition. Was that truly my reality as a child of God? It certainly felt like reality.

OVERCOMING ADVERSITY THROUGH MIRACLES

This family creed led me to be driven to success. I graduated *cum laude* from Loyola of Los Angeles and started a career in the healthcare industry. My parents had very little education and rewarded me with recognition for my success in college. I craved getting more "love" from them and having them proud of me.

I rapidly progressed up the ranks of corporate America and became Senior Vice President of a Fortune 25 company. I worked and worked and worked. I felt compelled to be successful and financially well off to receive love from those closest to me and from the world.

At 28 years of age, I had a spiritual conversion and started the journey of understanding—my reality wasn't about being successful in the world but to be faithful in the eyes of God.

One of the representatives on my staff—I was a Pharmaceutical District Manager—showed up at a meeting in Bakersfield, California, one day with a Holy Spirit pin. He was a worldly Catholic, kind of a "hell raiser." I knew he went to church but didn't really believe in Christ.

I said to him, "What's with the pin? Catholics don't wear Holy Spirit pins!" He told me that he had been "born again" and had given his life to Jesus!

That encounter impacted me greatly. Shook me to the core. I was very involved in our parish life. My wife and I taught religious education. We went to church regularly. But…if you were to follow me around, could I be convicted of being Christian?

I realized God was in my head, not in my heart. I prayed and God showed me that I didn't truly believe in him. I saw that my faith was cultural with little impact on my actions at work or with my family. (This moment of self-awareness led me, later in my life, to establish the "Spirit Filled Hearts Ministry.")

I drove the 150 miles from Bakersfield to Irvine where I lived. By the time I arrived home, I had made a decision to give Jesus my heart.

I was alone in the house and in my bedroom. I will never forget it. Standing before my reflection in the mirrored closet doors, I looked deeply into my eyes and uttered a short fervent prayer. "Lord, I give you my heart. Totally, completely and eternally. Use me in any way you want. I devote my life to you. I love you. Teach me to love you more."

I learned later opening my soul to the Lord is called a "fervent prayer." One from the heart. The "good thief on the cross" type of prayer. Fervent prayer can't be faked. It will be tested, but God will honor the prayer if it is truly from the heart. I meant it on that important day in my life.

Suddenly, everything changed. I mean everything. Instantly. Incredible! I walked from the bedroom into the living room. There, sitting on a table, was a huge white book with pictures. It had never been opened. Do

OVERCOMING ADVERSITY THROUGH MIRACLES

you know what that book was? During my talks, I ask audience members that question, and everyone gets it right: The Bible!

I was led to this holy book like a bee to honey. I opened it, and suddenly the scripture came alive. The verses literally leapt off the page. Why hadn't I heard this before? I had, but it was only head knowledge then, in one ear and out the other.

The first scripture I opened to was in the gospel of John.

> John 3:16 "For God so loved the world that he gave his only begotten Son, so that everyone who believes in him might not perish but have eternal life."

Wow! God so loved me that all I had to do was believe he was real, and God would be with me forever?

I then went to Paul's letter to the Romans.

> Romans 8:1 "Hence, now there is no condemnation for those in Christ Jesus."

Wow again! I had felt condemned my whole life. Not living up to expectations of my parents, wife, friends, boss, etc. Constantly striving to be perfect. Being a "people pleaser." It was never enough! But, if God didn't condemn me, why should I condemn myself?

I then read further in Romans.
> Romans 8 14-17, "For those who are led by

> the Spirit of God are children of God. For you do not receive a spirit of slavery to fall back into fear, but you received a spirit of adoption, through which we cry, 'Abba, Father!' The Spirit itself bears witness with our spirit that we are children of God, and if children, then heirs, of God and joint heirs with Christ, if we only we suffer with him so that we may also be glorified with him."

Wow! Wow! Wow! I am a child of God! So intimate with the Father, that I can say "Daddy?" That I will be glorified with him!

I continued to read more.

> Romans 8:35, 38 "What will separate us from the love of Christ? Will anguish, or distress, or persecution, or famine, or nakedness, or peril, or the sword? For I am convinced that neither death, nor life, nor angels, nor principalities, nor present things, nor future things, nor powers, nor height, nor depth, nor any other creature will be able to separate us from the love of God in Christ Jesus our Lord."

At this point, I was shaking. I began to pray fervently within me. I read further.

> Romans 8: 26-27 "In the same way, the Spirit too comes to the aid of our weakness; for we do not know how to pray as we ought, but the Spirit itself intercedes with inexpressible

> groaning. And the one who searches hearts knows what is the intention of the Spirit, because it intercedes for the holy ones according to God's will."

As, I read this passage, my eyes were opened. I started praying in a strange tongue. I did not realize until later that I had received the gift of "tongues." I was praying in the Spirit! I felt warm throughout my body, soul and spirit.

Next, I turned to the letter to the people of Ephesus.

> Ephesians 1:3-5 "Blessed be the God and Father of our Lord Jesus Christ, who has blessed us in Christ with every spiritual blessing in the heavens, as he chose us in him, before the foundation of the world, to be holy and without blemish before him. In love he destined us for adoption for himself through Jesus Christ, in accord with the favor of his will, for the praise of the glory of his grace that he granted us in the beloved."

You must be kidding! I was holy? Without blemish? God's adopted son? I have every spiritual blessing!

For the first time, in my heart, I understood God loved ME!!!! Unconditionally! I had a purpose: to tell others about Jesus! And that is exactly what I did. I couldn't put down the Bible. Each day, I read the Bible for 8-10 hours. I shared my new faith, my new reality of understanding God's love, with everyone I came across.

My parents, brothers, family, friends, strangers, co-workers…everyone!

After a few months, my mother called me one day and said she urgently needed to see me. I drove from Irvine to Glendale, California, and sat down on her couch in the living room.

"Steven," she said loudly and forcefully, "tell me the truth, you joined a cult! No one who is Catholic knows the Bible and talks about it all the time."

I felt she was going to ask me next what flavor Kool Aid I had drunk.

She didn't believe I was living out my Catholic faith—my Baptism to be Priest, Prophet and King. She instructed me to see the family priest, my cousin in San Diego.

Dutifully, my wife and I traveled down to San Diego and were examined. My cousin the priest affirmed I was okay, but suggested that I read books on the saints as well as the Bible.

My friends, I learned that God loved me. No matter what I did or didn't do. To this day, this realization gets me through trials and adversity.

I often ask people in my talks, "Does God love you more when you are good and not sinning?" Most people nod their heads and believe that is indeed the case: God loves us more when we don't sin. Don't fall into that trap! God loves us the same always and will love us always.

When we sin, we block God's blessings and reject his love. That is the fundamental issue—not that God loves us less, but rather that we are not open to receive his love.

When experiencing a trial, if we meditate and pray even more to open up our hearts to receive his love, the problems and challenges of life melt away in the bountiful sea of his love. We begin to realize at our core—our heart and our soul—we are not alone. God is here. Protecting us. Loving us. Guiding us.

Rejoice! We are adopted sons and daughters of God and are loved unconditionally for all of eternity!

CHAPTER 5

BAPTISM OF THE HOLY SPIRIT

God doesn't us to be alone or to feel abandoned, so God sent us the holy Spirit. In times of trial and challenge, we can draw upon the Spirit for help. The best request, by far, is to ask for the spiritual gifts integral to what is commonly called, "the baptism of the Holy Spirit."

The concept of being "baptized in the holy Spirit" is usually associated with spiritual gifts and the empowerment of Christian ministry. Jesus taught us, according to the author of the book of Acts:

> Acts 1:5 "For John baptized with water, but in a few days you will be baptized with the holy Spirit."

In Acts, we also learn the importance of forgiveness of sin.
> Acts 2:38 "Peter [said] to them, 'Repent and be baptized, every one of you, in the name of

Jesus Christ, for the forgiveness of your sins; and you will receive the gift of the holy Spirit."

The Catholic Church teaches that spiritual gifts "are endowments given by the holy Spirit. They are the supernatural graces that individual Christians need to fulfill the mission of the Church." In my opinion, these spiritual gifts are not optional but required to help us build up the church.

> 1 Corinthians 12:7 "To each individual the manifestation of the Spirit is given for some benefit."

We further see that the gifts are distributed individually, based upon the will of God.

> 1 Corinthians 12:11 "But one in the same Spirit produces all of these, distributing them individually to each person as he wishes."

During the sacrament of Baptism, when we receive the anointing of Sacred Chrism to be priest, prophet and king, we receive the authority to embody God's power.

> 1 Corinthians 4:20 "For the kingdom of God is not a matter of talk but power."

How do we release this power every day? It starts with loving God with all our hearts, souls, might and strength. We must desire to do God's will.

> Matthew 6:33 "But seek first the kingdom of

[God] and his righteousness, and all these things will be given you besides."

I have found that three important steps are required to receive the power God has preordained for us as Catholic Christians. The first is to request, in sincere and complete trust, that God use us according to his will. When we ask him in faith, we can be assured we have received the grace required to do the will of the Father.

> James 1:5-6 "But if any of you lacks wisdom, he should ask God who gives it to all generously and ungrudgingly, and he will be given it. But he should ask in faith, not doubting, for the one who doubts is like a wave of the sea that is driven and tossed about by the wind."

The letter of St. James further teaches that if we are to be true warriors for Christ, we must ask in a way pleasing to God.

> James 4:2-3 "You covet but do not possess. You kill and envy but you cannot obtain; you fight and wage war. You do not possess because you do not ask. You ask but do not receive, but because you ask wrongly, to spend it on your passions."

The second critical step to empowerment is to cultivate a true hunger for it.

> Matthew 5:6 "Blessed are they who hunger and thirst for righteousness, / for they will

be satisfied."

What do you hunger and thirst for? For many, it is health, finances, fruitful relationships and happiness. All these things are good; they are not enough to achieve the purpose for which God created us: to first know, love and serve him.

The final step in achieving God's power is to expect God has granted it to you. If we have the gift of faith, and do not doubt, God honors our belief.

> James 1:7-8 "For that person must not suppose that he will receive anything from the Lord, since he is a man of two minds, unstable in all his ways."

When we surrender to the love of Jesus, we are filled with the Holy Spirit and can be certain he has given us spiritual gifts. Strengthened with these gifts, we can set the earth on fire with the love of Jesus.

> Luke 12:49: "I have come to set the earth of fire, and how I wish it were already blazing!"

Paul's letter to the Corinthians describes nine spiritual gifts of the Spirit.

> 1 Corinthians 12:8-10 "To one is given through the Spirit the expression of wisdom; to another the expression of knowledge according to the same Spirit; to another faith by the same Spirit; to another gifts of healing by the one Spirit; to another mighty deeds; to

another prophecy; to another discernment of spirits; to another varieties of tongues; to another interpretations of tongues."

These gifts are critical instruments to achieve what God wants for our church. They are also essential to provide us strength in overcoming the adversities that come with trials. These gifts are divided into three groups: word, sign and revelation.

The "word gifts" enable the believer to receive the powers of prophesy, speaking in tongues and interpretation of tongues.

Prophesy is a supernaturally inspired utterance from God meant to build up the Body of Christ. This gift of the Spirit reveals the mind of God.

> 1 Corinthians 14:1-3 "Pursue love, but strive eagerly for the spiritual gifts, above all that you may prophesy. For one who speaks in a tongue does not speak to human beings but to God, for no one listens; he utters mysteries in spirit. On the other hand, one who prophesies does speak to human beings, for their building up, encouragement, and solace."

Prophecy builds up and bears fruit!

The second word gift is the gift of tongues, an ability. mentioned 57 times in the New Testament and 12 times in 1 Corinthians 14 alone! This gift was used by the church extensively in the first 2½ centuries.

How do we define speaking in tongues? It is praising God through prayer language or an actual language. I have heard said that speaking in tongues is God within you praying with God the Father!

Modern-day scholars estimate some 5,000 live languages exist today, with a recognized 1,000-plus dead languages <u>and</u> angelic languages.

A number of years ago, I had an incredible experience at a prayer meeting. A woman, who had driven for more than an hour to attend the meeting, was rear-ended on the freeway on the way. She experienced a whiplash and suffered pain in her neck and shoulder.

As I went to pray over her, she told me the story of what happened. I felt bad for her and begin praying in the Spirit fervently in a language I had never prayed in before or since. After a short time, the woman became very emotional. Crying, she looked up at me. Her pain had disappeared, but that was not the cause of her emotional state.

She told me, "Deacon Steve, I need to tell the prayer group what happened."

She then stood up and announced to the group, "Deacon Steve just prayed over me in ancient Arabic, in the language of Jesus. He was praying the Lord's prayer!"

Wow! The woman was from the Middle East and knew Arabic, the language I had spoken in prayer. Everyone began praising God for his goodness. Whatever challenges we had melted away in the love of Christ!

The gift of tongues gives power because, at times, we don't know how to pray as we need to.

> Romans 8:26-27 "The Spirit too comes to the aid of our weakness; for we do not know how to pray as we ought, but the Spirit intercedes with inexpressible groanings... It intercedes for the holy ones."

The gift of tongues comes in four forms: praying (man to God), singing, speaking (God to man), and a sign to the unsaved as described in Corinthians.

> 1 Corinthians 14:22 "Thus, tongues are a sign not for those who believe but for unbelievers."

There are four levels of tongues: sublinguistic (childlike babble); actual language; jubilis, a form of Yodel; and deep mystical prayer, ecstatic utterance often used by monks over the centuries.

In the 16th century, tongues were expressed in the church 20 minutes before the gospel and 20 minutes after communion! How awesome was that! Church members often would sing in tongues, which always brings great power to the community.

What is the purpose of the gift of tongues with respect to overcoming adversity? First, it helps drive out demonic influence and is often used in deliverance prayer. I highly recommend it when you feel attacked and are in a spiritual battle.

I have been in the healing ministry for more 40 years and find speaking in tongues is an essential element of healing prayer. Whenever I pray over someone, I use tongues as the foundation of my prayer, which usually leads to "words of knowledge" and encourages the person being prayed over. I don't know what I am saying, but I feel the love and power of the holy Spirit when I pray in the Spirit.

The story of my daughter when she was five years old illustrates the use of the gift of tongues in times of crisis or trial. My brothers and I were all together, and my daughter was chasing her cousin through the house. When the cousin went into the kitchen, she opened the sliding glass door, then closed it behind herself.

Somehow, my daughter didn't see her close the door and went running straight through the plate glass door. I was in another room and heard a huge crash. I instantly started to pray.

My wife and I went running to our daughter. Neither of us said a word. My daughter's face was covered with blood. Cuts all over her body. Eventually, her face would require more than 300 stitches. We prayed nonstop in tongues for hours—waiting for the ambulance, in the ambulance, and the three-plus hours in the hospital waiting room while the plastic surgeon worked to repair the damage to our daughter's face. Persistent prayer in the Spirit gave us tremendous peace in this time of trial.

When the plastic surgeon came out finally and saw us, he shook his head. All he could say was he had never seen anything like it. He said our daughter never cried and was perfect the whole time. The biggest miracle? Despite needing more than 300 stitches to repair the lacerations, not a single muscle or tendon had been damaged! Praise God! Now and forever!

If you don't have the gift of tongues, ask for it! Expect to receive it. When you do receive the gift, use it often. It will help you greatly in times of trial.

Interpretation of tongues, the third "word" gift of the holy Spirit, is rarely seen. Spoken aloud in prayer meetings, it is a message from God to his people. Someone in the prayer community must ask and expect to receive the gift of interpreting what is said for the community.

The next set of spiritual gifts are often referred to as "sign" gifts, which empower the believer to perform certain acts. These gifts include faith, healing and miracles.

The Lord always gives us the gift of faith when we ask, as demonstrated many times in scripture. This supernatural gift of faith can be described as "I know that I know that I know." God gives us this sense of certainty. Faith gives us the strength to endure trials. I will examine faith in greater detail later.

The next sign gift is healing. In Mark's gospel, Jesus tells us the importance of healing.
    Mark 16:17-18 "These signs will accompany

those who believe: in my name they will drive out demons, they will speak new languages. They will pick up serpents [with their hands], and if they drink any deadly thing, it will not harm them. They will lay hands on the sick, and they will recover."

A friend of mine had a massive tumor in his lung and was given a 1 in 500 chances of survival. We decided to turn to God's mercy and healing, praying through the power of the holy Spirit and the intercession of the Blessed Mother. During our prayers, my friend said he felt fire travel throughout his body.

Upon examining my friend two weeks later, the doctor couldn't believe that he found no trace of cancer. He sent the tissue to the Mayo Clinic, and it came back totally clear of cancer. Praise God! This trial and adversity was overcome with the miracle and love of Jesus and the Blessed Mother!

The final sign gift is miracles, defined as "passing manifestations of God's power whereby some obstacle is removed or some opportunity is seized in a very special way, so that it could only come from God's intervention into human affairs."

I totally believe in miracles. As I write these words, this very evening I experienced a miracle.

We had gathered with nearly 300 young adults in Christ Cathedral in the Diocese of Orange, to praise and worship God. Earlier in the evening, I had prayed over a woman in a wheel chair. As the night drew to a close, the woman made her way to the front, and we, as a group, began to pray over her.

The Lord told me she was to raise herself out of the wheel chair—something she hadn't done in years. I asked if she wanted to stand. At first, she wasn't sure, but then the Holy Spirit took over. The woman stood for the first time in years, and I could see her back, once weak and curved, suddenly become strong and straightened. She began to weep and all in the theater began singing, "Alleluia! Amen!" Yet another miracle!

The next set of spiritual gifts are the revelation gifts: wisdom, knowledge and discernment of spirits.

Wisdom is an insight into God's plan in a given situation, meant to be put it into action. Wisdom is one of the traditional seven gifts of the holy Spirt found in Isaiah 11. When we ask for wisdom, we can be assured that, like Solomon, we will receive it.

The word of knowledge is a gift of a supernatural revelation of facts—present and future—from the Lord. This gift is used to build up the person and show him or her how to draw closer to Christ. We see the word of knowledge manifested in a verse in John's gospel.

> John 16:13 "When he comes, the Spirit of truth, he will guide you to all truth. He will not speak on his own, but he will speak what he hears, and will declare to you the things that are coming."

The word of knowledge can be manifested in words,

songs, teaching or scripture.

The final gift is discernment of spirits, which enables a person to know the source of an inspiration or action—whether the source is the holy Spirit, the human spirit or an evil spirit. With this gift, we can ascertain what is controlling thoughts, actions and even people themselves. Pray fervently for this gift, always a critical support, especially during times of trial.

God intends us to have the power to overcome adversity and trials. He gives us many spiritual gifts to strengthen us!

CHAPTER 6

EXPECTANT FAITH

Faith is mentioned more than 200 times in the Bible. Faith moves mountains. Faith transforms us into the image of Christ.

When we are going through trials and tribulations, our human nature wants to control the situation, fix it and make it go away. What does God want for us? His desire is for us to trust him. "Jesus, I Trust In You!"

My spiritual director encouraged me to say "Jesus, I Trust In You" on every bead of the rosary when I am in a state of despair. It is important to use contemplative prayer and meditation when we fear, rather than let the fear disable us. Look for your own "prayer closet" with the Lord—a special place in your home, garden, etc. that you choose for prayer—and spend time in contemplation or meditation. Through prayer, we are transformed and receive the peace and love God wants for us.

> John 14:27 "Peace I leave with you; my peace I give to you. Not as the world gives do I give it to you. Do not let your hearts be troubled or afraid."

How in the world can we receive this peace when we feel as if everything is crashing down on us? I believe achieving peace of heart and mind is impossible from a human standpoint. However, with God all things are possible.

What do we know about faith? It is essential to please God.

> Hebrews 11:6 "But without faith it is impossible to please him, for anyone who approaches God must believe he exists and that he rewards those who seek him."

In other words, no matter how many spiritual works or works of mercy we perform, rosaries we pray, prayers we utter, Masses we attend or anything else, if we do not believe in Jesus, trust him and call to him, we do not please him.

How do we develop this kind of faith? The faith of the Centurion? We must ask for it!

We read in scripture that faith comes from listening.

> Romans 10:17 "Thus faith comes from what is heard, and what is heard comes through the word of Christ."

To receive what God is telling us, we must desire,

listen and expect him to speak to us. People tell me so often they never hear God speak to them. I believe they have not asked for faith and do not expect God to give them faith. God does not say "Yes" and then, "No." Jesus promised the Holy Spirit would teach us what we need to know to increase our faith and to understand what God wants for our lives.

> John 14:26 "The Advocate, the holy Spirit that the Father will send in my name—he will teach you everything and remind you of all that [I] told you."

To have expectant faith means we are waiting for God to reveal his grace and blessings to us, no matter what the circumstance. Paul defines faith as this hopeful waiting in his letter to the Hebrews.

> Hebrews 11:1 "Faith is the realization of what is hoped for and evidence of things not seen."

A powerful verse follows this passage.

> Hebrews 11:3 "By faith we understand that the universe was ordered by the word of God, so that what is visible came into being through the invisible."

Reflecting on this scripture, we realize our faith, through God, makes the realities in our lives happen.

A good story about expectant faith occurred during one of our ministry pilgrimages to the Holy Land. A woman on the trip suffered from a severely dislocated shoulder, which had happened several days before our departure. She could barely lift up her right arm. She obviously was in tremendous pain. At one of the holy sites, I could see her struggling. I prayed fervently, asking God to perform a miracle.

When it comes to expectant faith, I often think of the two blind men in Matthew's gospel.

> Matthew 9:27-29 "And as Jesus passed on from there, two blind men followed [him], crying out, 'Son of David, have pity on us!' When he entered the house, the blind men approached him and Jesus said to them, 'Do you believe that I can do this?' 'Yes, Lord' they said to him. Then he touched their eyes and said, 'Let it be done for you according to your faith.'"

Recalling this scripture, I asked the woman, "Do you believe that God can heal you?"

I will never forget as long as I live the expression on her face. I could tell she was processing whether or not she believed. I saw her entire face change as she enthusiastically answered me, "I believe!"

At that moment, my faith expanded tremendously and "I knew that I knew that I knew." God was going to do something incredible. I called upon God's merciful grace and healing power to mend her shoulder instantly. I had no doubt. I totally believed! The woman totally believed!

Within 30 seconds, the woman was screaming, laughing and saying repeatedly, "I believe!" With her once-dislocated shoulder, she thrust her arm into the air, shouting again and again, "I believe, I believe!"

As I travel throughout this country and the world, I experience and feel the suffering of so many. People pray and ask for help, but nothing seems to change. I believe one significant reason for a seeming lack of response from God is many people simply don't expect anything to change. Their focus is on their problem; their eyes are not set on Jesus. Like Peter walking on the water, they look at their trials—the waves—and fail to focus on Christ. When we walk, we must walk in faith and not by what we see.

> 2 Corinthians 5:7 "For we walk by faith, not by sight."

In my talks, I often hold up the Bible and ask audience members what would happen if I dropped the holy book. Would it rise up in the air, hover? Of course not! One-hundred percent of the people—and you—know the answer. It would come crashing to the floor due to the physical law of gravity.

We clearly understand physical laws but fail to realize spiritual laws of God. When we ask for faith, we will get it! When we desire more faith and ask for it, we are assured our Father will give us the faith to move mountains.

> Matthew 17:20 "Amen, I say to you, if you have faith the size of a mustard seed, you will say to this mountain, 'Move from here to

there,' and it will move. Nothing will be impossible for you."

Most of us struggle to understand spiritual laws. We don't understand that having and using spiritual gifts is normal Christianity. The "abundant life" that Jesus promised us. It is why we can rest in him. Take his yoke upon us—for it is easy—and know that we are loved. We are not alone.

CHAPTER 7

WINNING THE BATTLEFIELD OF THE MIND

We are at war. We may not see our adversaries or realize they are battling us, but they are real nevertheless. We base draw our strength on the Lord and draw upon his power.

> Ephesians 6:10-13 "Finally, draw your strength from the Lord and from his mighty power. Put on the armor of God so that you may be able to stand firm against the tactics of the devil. For our struggle is not with flesh and blood but with the principalities, with the powers, with the world rulers of this present darkness, with the evil spirits in the heavens. Therefore, put on the armor of God, that you may be able to resist on the evil day and, having done everything, to hold your ground."

Our enemy attacks our weaknesses. When we feel

powerless, out of control, not knowing how to get past our problems, we open ourselves to the enemy's discouragement, which could lead to sin.

Drawing upon the Lord's strength means we are confident he will give us his strength.

> Philippians 4:13 "I have the strength for everything through him who empowers me."

God knows our needs before we open our mouths. He provides what we need as the loving Father he is.

> Philippians 4:19 "My God will fully supply whatever you need, in accord with his glorious riches in Christ Jesus."

Psychologists tell us that each day we encounter 2,000 choices and decisions. Are we moving toward God or away from God in those choices? We must realize God wants to protect us, and the enemy desires to weaken us and defeat God's purpose for our lives.

> 1 Peter 5:8 "Be sober and vigilant. Your opponent the devil is prowling around like a roaring lion looking for [someone] to devour."

Similar to Peter's choice to deny Christ during the Passion, the devil wants us to choose the flesh and the world.

Satan is a liar. He often tells us we are junk and unloved and that trials will always beset us. The devil tries to convince us there is no God and we can never be forgiven. Lies!

Learning how to win this war with evil is critical. In fact, we must understand God has already won the war. When we are obedient to God and resist the devil, he will flee from us.

> James 4:7 "Resist the devil, and he will flee from you."

God is within us, and he is infinitely greater than any force against us!

> 1 John 4:4 "…for the one who is in us is greater than the one who is in the world."

Winning this battle with the enemy takes seven steps.

First, we can't be double-minded, distracted by the world and our busy lives.

> James 1:7-8 "We must not suppose that we will receive anything if we are a man of two minds, unstable in all his ways."

It is time we take seriously our faith and totally surrender to Christ. I often say our greatest and most difficult journey is just 18 inches—from our heads to our hearts. How much do we hunger and thirst for God? We know Jesus said he thirsts for us and for our souls. Would we do anything for him? Sacrifice for him? Deny ourselves for him? Die for him?

When we surrender to God, we put him first and foremost. Doing so removes the power posed by trials and challenges. We become indifferent to them; Christ becomes our priority!

Our second step in winning this battle is to ask the holy Spirit to take over our lives and lead us. I find it powerful that the holy Spirit leads us into battle against Satan.

> Matthew 4:1 "The Jesus was led by the Spirit into the desert to be tempted by the devil."

Without the holy Spirit, we cannot draw upon the Spirit's gifts and fruits, essential to defeat the enemy.

The third step and spiritual tool is to ask for faith.

> 1 Peter 5:9 "Resist him, steadfast in faith."

Faith is our shield. Faith protects us against the devil's attacks.

> Ephesians 6:16 "In all circumstances, hold faith as a shield, to quench all [the] flaming arrows of the evil one."

Faith gives us the strength, peace and joy to overcome whatever is sent against us.

The fourth step in battling evil is to use praise and prayers to strengthen us and rout the enemy. God inhabits the praises of his people as Psalm 22 proclaims. When we pray "in the Spirit" or tongues, we pray directly to the Father in a way that we can't comprehend, but doing so gives us grace and strength. Other tools are praying the blood of Jesus over your family, friends, people you are praying for and with and yourself. The precious blood of Jesus protects and purifies the person or individual whom you pray it upon. The same blood that poured from the side of Jesus at his crucifixion is the blood of Salvation. We must recognize the importance of the eternal cup of salvation is for us, and we can use this spiritual tool to pray for people. It is extremely important! I have 40 years of experience with healing and spiritual warfare that attests to that reality.

In addition, ask for protection from your guardian angel and especially Saint Michael the Archangel. Pray the litany to Saint Michael.

Finally, pray and say the name of Jesus. At times, I pronounce the name of Jesus over and over until the attack passes.

> Luke 10:17 "Lord even the demons are subject to us because of your name."
>
> Mark 16:17 "In my name they will drive out demons."

Remember the truth of these words:

> Philippians 2:9 "Because of this, God greatly exalted him / and bestowed on him the name / that is above every name, / that at the name of Jesus / every knee should bend, / of those in heaven and one earth and under the earth, / and every tongue confess that / Jesus Christ is Lord, / to the

glory of the Father."

The fifth step, also extremely important, is to use spiritual tools to strengthen us against attacks and provide support in our trials. The sacraments are the most vital of these tools, beginning with the sacrament of Reconciliation. I can't overemphasize the importance of Reconciliation. We enter the confessional broken and full of shame and leave confident, healed and full of grace.

Please take advantage of this critical sacrament, which provides tremendous protection against the enemy's attacks by giving us grace to defend us. The attacks seem to just melt away, in my experience. How often should we seek the sacrament of Reconciliation? Often! You decide for yourself, but at least once per month and many times twice—not that we are stubborn sinners as much as we want the sacrament's grace to enable us to fulfill our individual purpose and mission.

The next spiritual tool is the most important: the Mass and Eucharist. For years, my spiritual director told me to attend to daily Mass. Like many of us, I came up with excuse after excuse. The reality? There is no excuse! If it is important, you will find a way to go to Mass, if not daily then as often as possible during the week. We need to receive this "daily bread" to strengthen and fill us with grace and love!

Other spiritual tools include participating in a prayer meeting. Do not isolate yourself. When in the midst of trials, we often don't want to see or talk to anyone. I remember wanting to pull the sheets and blankets over my head and not get out of bed. This tendency to isolation plays directly into the hands of the enemy. Go to Mass, prayer meetings, adoration and bible studies. Be led by the Spirit. In addition, fast on a regular basis. We know that fasting strengthens our prayers.

The sixth step in winning the battle of the mind is to take every thought captive.

> 2 Corinthians 10:4-5 "For the weapons of our battle are not of flesh but are enormously powerful, capable of destroying fortresses. We destroy arguments and every pretension raising itself against the knowledge of God and take every thought captive in obedience to Christ."

It is so critical and important, is this battlefield response. Like a finely tuned athlete, we must train and become disciplined. Memorize this important verse:

> Philippians 4:8 "Whatever is true, whatever is honorable, whatever is just, whatever is pure, whatever is lovely, whatever is gracious, if there is any excellence and if there is anything worthy of praise, think about these things."

Let only things of the Lord enter your mind. This includes what you read, what you watch on television., what you view on your computer or smart phone. No compromise. None! If someone speaks negatively about anything or anyone, either change the conversation or leave. When we are under trial and adversity, the enemy wants to discourage us. He attacks our minds. Win the battlefield of the mind and we win the battle and, ultimately, the war.

The final step to strengthen us on this battlefield is performing spiritual and corporate works of mercy. To what extent are we involved in spreading the word of God? Helping the poor with their challenges? Do we work with those in leadership in our parishes? What leadership roles can we take within our parish and even the Diocese?

In summary, renounce Satan and he will flee from you. Use the power and name of Jesus. Be involved in church through the sacraments and make a difference in building the body of Christ. Do not let the enemy in the door with unconfessed sin. Take the authority God has given us through our Baptism to defeat the attacks of the devil. Be single-minded, focusing on Jesus as our solution. Avoid sexual sin, pride, self-righteousness, lack of forgiveness, bitterness, anger, resentment, revenge, violence, self-condemnation and anxiety.

In times of trial, powerful tools are available to defeat the enemy. Learn how to use them often and daily. You will receive such grace and strength you never knew possible.

Praise the Lord! Now and forever!

CHAPTER 8

LIVING THE MERCY OF CHRIST

When it feels as if the sky is falling in and the end is near; when we are close to giving up, then, most of all, we must ask for and cling to God's mercy.

If understanding in our hearts that unconditional love is difficult without God's supernatural intervention, then grasping God's mercy is equally challenging. What is mercy? It is defined by our church as "the loving kindness, compassion, or forbearance shown to one who offends."

The word "mercy" appears in scripture 149 times. We know, most of us, the Beatitude in Matthew's gospel.

> Matthew 5:7 "Blessed are the merciful, / for they will be shown mercy."

The Father wants us to be instruments of mercy.

> Luke 6:36 "Be merciful, just as [also] your Father is merciful."

In the Old Testament, God's mercy is explained in in the book of Exodus.

> Exodus 34:6 "So the LORD passed before him, and proclaimed: The LORD, the LORD, a God gracious and merciful, slow to anger and abounding in love and fidelity."

Mercy is closely related to God's love. I believe it is the cousin of love. Because of God's love, we receive God's mercy. To endure trials and hardships, we must remember that we are not alone. The first step is to be open in our hearts to receive this truth: the all-merciful God loves us passionately and completely, for all of eternity.

Please take time to meditate before the Blessed Sacrament and open your heart to receive the love of Christ. When we do that, we gain the strength and courage to withstand the enemy's attacks and ease our own doubts and fears to find hope. When we hope, we are transformed by the love of Jesus. When we love God, we dwell in his presence.

> John 14:23 "Whoever loves me will keep my word, and my Father will love him, and we will come to him and make our dwelling with him."

It is interesting to me that when I am in the greatest pain and adversity, God gives me the greatest opportunity to spread the word of God. Sharing my faith with others is a critical part of giving mercy. My attitude of despair changes immediately when I begin to share my faith in joy regarding the good news of Jesus Christ—his mercy, forgiveness of sin and redemption. I see the looks on people's faces as I tell them, "There is no condemnation for those who love Christ Jesus." Their own pain begins to change as they accept the mercy of Christ.

I had a job that often required me to fly "red-eye" flights from Los Angeles International to Boston's Logan airport, landing about 5:30 a.m. Grumpy and full of complaining, I would get off the plane and start my long walk to the rental car office.

Along the way, I would pass by a man shining shoes. I got in the habit of stopping and having him work on my shoes. We would talk about life and family. He was always in a great mood. I asked him why one day. His response?

"I always have a great day because each day I am devoted to help other people have a great day," he told me.

I have never forgotten that spiritual truth. Helping others to have a great day makes our troubles and challenges seem insignificant. When I share my faith, two people have a great day—the person to whom I speak and me. God's mercy and kindness flows through me.

Another step of mercy is fulfilling the purpose of our

lives. Each of us is called to be the hands, heart, mind and words of Jesus. We can achieve what God wants for us only by calling upon the release of the holy Spirit within us. The Holy Spirit leads us to the Spiritual and Corporal Works of Mercy.

The first Spiritual Work is "counseling the doubtful." We draw upon scripture to give us guidance in speaking with people.

> 1 Corinthians 1:25 "For the foolishness of God is wiser than human wisdom, and the weakness of God is stronger than human strength."

We don't need to explain things with human logic, but rather, we draw our strength from the holy Spirit. We let God speak through us.

The second Spiritual Work is "instructing the ignorant." We learn about our faith and are open to talk to others about what we believe and why. We must educate ourselves and use what we learn to be a blessing to others!

The next Spiritual Work of Mercy is "admonishing the sinner." Performing this work may feel as if we are judging others; however, it is actually about being the light of Christ to others. People openly sin. They may not fully appreciate that what they do is a sin. Our task is to share the truth —in love—about their actions. They will thank us for it!

The fourth Spiritual Work is "comforting the

sorrowful," which leads us back to the Beatitudes in Matthew's gospel

> Matthew 5:4 "Blessed are they who morn, / for they will be comforted."

We must be listeners, actively present to others. When we act in this way, we become Jesus to them! We reassure them that they are not alone, that we—as Jesus does—love and care about them!

"Forgiving injuries" is the next Spiritual Work of mercy. Forgiving injury may start within each of us. Have you forgiven yourself? Forgiving one's self is a struggle for many. And many of us wrestle with forgiving those who hurt us. We can carry grudges for years.

Forgiveness, a cornerstone of healing, transforms our hearts and minds. In the Lord's Prayer, we pray that we "must forgive those who trespass against us." The degree to which we forgive is the measure of how much we are forgiven.

The sixth Spiritual Work of mercy is "bearing wrongs patiently." Each of us is hurt and will be hurt by another. Often these hurts can lead to depression and a great deal of anxiety. What do we do? First, we pray for those who injure us. Second, we picture them with the eyes of Jesus. Are they loved by Jesus? Forgiven by Jesus? When we see others as Jesus does, our attitude changes, often immediately.

The final Spiritual Work of Mercy is "praying for the

living and the dead." I believe it is very important to build up our faith and defend ourselves against evil by praying fervently each day the Divine Mercy Chaplet and the rosary—surrendering to the love of Jesus, through the power of the holy Spirit, and to the love of the Blessed Mother. Our Blessed Mother is called "the Mother of Mercy." We ask for her intercession and her immaculate heart to fill us.

Recall what the Blessed Mother said to Saint Brigid of Sweden, "I am the Queen of heaven and the Mother of Mercy."

I encourage everyone to adopt the habit of praying daily for the souls in Purgatory, to intercede for them through praying the rosary and praising God for the people put into your heart to pray for daily.

When we focus on what God desires for our thoughts and actions, we are also led to the Corporal Works of Mercy. Saint Mother Teresa once said that we can be assured we will be examined upon death by the Lord according to what Jesus taught us.

> Matthew 25: 35-36, 40 "For I was hungry and you gave me food, I was thirsty and you gave me drink, a stranger and you welcomed me, naked and you clothed me, ill and you cared for me, in prison and you visited me. … Amen, I say to you, whatever you did for one of those least brothers of mine, you did for me."

The first Corporal Work of Mercy is to "feed the

hungry." Do you know people who are hungry? We don't have to look far to find them. My friend carries canned food in his car and, seeing those hungry in the streets, stops and gives them food. We go to the streets, homeless shelters, food pantries and everywhere in the world to feed those in need. Our worries melt away when we work for the Lord!

The second Corporal Work of mercy is "give drink to the thirsty." Billions of people around the world do not have access to clean water, a harsh reality, we, in our nation of wealth, find hard to fathom. Our ministry, Spirit Filled Hearts, partners with "Wells for Life," an organization dedicated to building 1,000 wells in Uganda. I am pleased we contributed and have been responsible for four of these urgently needed wells.

"Shelter the Homeless"—the third Corporal Work of mercy—is critical. So many people—men, women and children—live in cars or on the streets. We are responsible for the struggle to secure affordable housing and homeless shelters. It is not easy; however, to do nothing is not God's will. When we fight for those who have no one to fight for them—those on society's margins—we become Jesus in action! Guess what? We find ourselves filled with gratitude and not focused on our issues.

One of the most rewarding things for me is to "visit the sick." We can all practice this Corporal Work of mercy, beginning with learning who is sick. Ask your Pastor, Priest or Deacon for suggestions on whom to visit. Take along a companion, if feasible, and bring a smile, a rosary if possible, and your prayers! We have seen miracle after miracle when we visit the sick and those in need of God's love.

One recent example from my life concerned a young man who, following a serious car accident, was in a coma. When we saw him, not much hope remained for his recovery. But Jesus is the God of hope! We prayed a rosary over the young man, had expectant faith and believed in God's miracles.

We see so many miracles but somehow, someway, the wonder of them always knocks me off my feet. So, I was awestruck when we returned to see the young man. He had regained consciousness and was alert and fully functioning. As if the accident had never happened. Truly a miracle!

When we implement the Corporal Work of mercy, "visit the prisoners," we take the love of God into a place of suffering and pain. I was blessed to be involved with detention ministry—or "restorative justice"—for seven years. Each time I brought hope and Jesus with me. Every time, I saw the face of Jesus in those I ministered to as they, in turn, ministered to me.

An example of incredible love was demonstrated one visit as I prayed individually over each of several women inmates. When I reached one women in line to ask what she wanted me to pray for, she leaned over and whispered, "My bunkee who has no one to pray for her." Such incredible love!

"Bury the dead" and "give alms to the poor" are the

final two Corporal Works of Mercy. Find out if your church or parish has a bereavement ministry and join or start one. Comfort those hurting from the loss of loved ones.

Locate a charity to support with your time, talent and treasure. Make sure your money is actually going to services for the poor. There are so many worthy organizations. Help them make a difference!

The final thought regarding God's mercy is to pray "The Divine Mercy Chaplet" daily. This prayer helps us focus on those in need of Jesus' love and mercy. God will bless us tremendously. The Divine Mercy devotion helps and encourages us to consecrate our lives to Jesus and only Jesus. We receive his mercy and grow in holiness. We ask God to help us do his will by loving his people and being agents of his mercy.

Remember the ABCs of mercy: Ask for mercy, be merciful to others and Completely trust in Jesus.

When we focus on being an instrument of mercy and opening to receive mercy, our lives are transformed by the love of Jesus. We no longer concentrate on our own challenges and pain but on becoming part of the solution of hope and love to others!

CHAPTER 9

LIVING A LIFE OF HOPE

When we despair, hurting and in emotional pain, we often lose hope. We think things will never get better. A lie from the enemy! What is true is that God is with us every second we struggle in pain. He whispers in our ear to trust him.

One of the most encouraging of all scriptures is found in the book of the prophet Jeremiah.

> Jeremiah 29:11, "For I know well the plans I have in mind for you—oracle of the LORD—plans for your welfare and not for woe, so as to give you a future full of hope."

Why focus on a future the enemy wants us to believe is dark and awful? We have a Father in heaven who loves us beyond comprehension, who wants to give us "every spiritual blessing" as promised in the first chapter of Paul's letter to the Ephesians.

During my career, when I headed company sales operations, I created the "Ten Attributes of a Winner." The first one was "A winner becomes what they think about."

I believe life becomes a self-fulfilling prophecy. If I think I will be successful, I will find a way to be successful. If I think God loves me, is protecting me and keeping me safe, I will act accordingly. Our entire life and attitude is dramatically impacted by what we think about our future.

God wants us to be filled with his holy Spirit—filled so completely that our hearts soar toward heaven as we praise his name. We see this reflected in Isaiah's beautiful image of eagle wings.

> Isaiah 40:31, "They that hope in the LORD will renew their strength, / they will soar on eagles wings; / They will and run not grow weary, / walk and not grow faint."

Do you want to renew your strength? When we feel hopeless and full of dread, we are tired all the time, lacking the energy to simply move forward. When we believe in the future—believe something good is about to happen—our strength is renewed. We become "empowered" by the Lord to face whatever challenges we encounter in life. We meet them head on.

> Philippians 4:13 "I have the strength for everything through him who empowers me."

When we face trials, it often feels as if we are all alone.

No one is standing by our side. The weight of the world lies heavily on our shoulders. Once again, a lie from the enemy. What is true is that God is always there for us, helping us by guarding us.

We look for a "Superman" to watch over us and fly to our rescue. In reality, God is far greater than anything or anyone we can dream of. He watches over us and guards us from evil every moment.

> Psalm 121: 7-8, "The LORD will guard you from all evil; / he will guard your soul. / The LORD will guard your coming and going / both now and forever."

So much of life encompasses trusting in the Lord. The measure of our trust determines our level of anxiety and our degree of hope. If we believe God is on our side, that his promises in scripture of loving and protecting us against all evil are true, we do not let our problems overwhelm us.

> Hebrews 10:23 "Let us hold unwaveringly to our confession that gives us hope, for he who made the promise is trustworthy."

Understanding why we have to suffer is difficult. Why must we endure so many trials in our lives? If God loves us, doesn't he want to save us from all this pain and suffering? We ponder this great question from the depths of our human hearts.

But God's ways and God's thinking are far beyond our human comprehension. He has the big picture in mind. He wants to teach us endurance so whatever the world or the enemy throws against us will not penetrate our defenses and defeat us. He seeks to build our character so we become warriors to win souls for him.

> Romans 5: 3-5, "Not only that, but we even boast of our afflictions, knowing that affliction produces endurance, and endurance, proven character, and proven character, hope, and hope does not disappoint, because the love of God has been poured out into our hearts through the holy Spirit that has been given to us."

One of our biggest challenges and battles is the desire for immediate "change" in our lives. We want to be totally and completely in charge of what happens in our lives. In our impatience, we pray and nothing happens because God is teaching us a fruit of the holy Spirit: patience.

Patience is demanding. It is difficult, often like a vise around our head, body and soul that seems too much to bear. Yet, God's word gives us many promises. When we wait on the Lord, he will deliver in due time, according to his grace. Try resting in God and the promises in the word of God.

> Psalm 130:5, "I wait for the LORD, / my soul waits and I hope for his word."

Understanding that we represent Christ is an important reality of being hope-filled people. Do we depict hope in our lives or fear? Do others look at us when we are in the midst of trials and see confidence and belief that God is with us and helps us endure our suffering?

Many people, like my wife and me, have had major challenges with their children and loved ones. Hope is difficult when we receive horrific news regarding someone we love.

That happened to us when my daughter called to tell us she had lung cancer. Lung Cancer? She never had even taken a puff of a cigarette. Didn't even drink at all. Yet, our only daughter is given this challenge. The news became even worse when she called and said the cancer had entered her heart, and she felt she wasn't going to survive.

When we face these challenges, we have two major choices: we can move toward God (consolation) or away from God (desolation). As for my wife and me, we chose then, and continue to choose, moving toward God.

People frequently ask how I can remain so calm in the middle of this crisis. So confident in the Lord. The reason is my hope in the Lord. The Apostle Peter explains it well.

> 1 Peter 3:13-17 "Now who is going to harm you if you are enthusiastic for what is good? But even if you should suffer because of righteousness, blessed are you. Do not be afraid or terrified with fear of them, but sanctify Christ as Lord in your hearts. Always be ready to give an explanation to anyone who asks you for a reason for your hope, but do it with gentleness and reverence, keeping

your conscience clear, so that, when you are maligned, those who defame your good conduct in Christ may themselves be put to shame. For it is better to suffer for doing good, if that be the will of God, than for doing evil."

When you feel hopeless, think of God's great love for you—you, your family, friends and everyone! Open your hearts to receive the hope that will never disappoint—God's everlasting hope.

When others would lament and give up, our hope-filled spirit in crisis becomes a great witness to friends and family and the world. When the God of hope takes over our lives, we enjoy the peace that passes all understanding. Peace the world can't give us.

Guard your hearts and minds against sin during times of trial. For me, difficult times are opportunities to draw closer to the Lord through daily Mass and frequent reception of the sacrament of reconciliation.

The devil wants us to give up and give in to our flesh. Often, people may turn to drinking, immorality or other forms of pleasure to numb the pain of suffering. Be on guard against the tricks of the devil. Instead of turning toward the world, turn to Jesus. You will never regret it!

CHAPTER 10

HEALING OF MEMORIES

When we try hard to overcome trials, memories of past challenges come flooding back into our minds, and we think, "No, not this again!" The devil tries to get us to focus on the memory and not the Lord. Once again, the "father of lies" strikes again. The important and consoling truth is that we are a new creation in Christ.

> 2 Corinthians 5:17 "So whoever is in Christ is a new creation: the old things have passed away; behold, new things have come."

Jesus is our Savior, our Redeemer and our Healer. When a memory causes us to lose hope, turn away from God or even sin, we must give that memory to God for healing. Rather than numbing the pain with self-destructive thoughts and actions or ignoring it and burying it deep in our consciousness, put Jesus at the center of it. When a dark memory comes to us, put Jesus in the scene of what happened.

For example, being in the room with my mother when she took her last breath was so painful. She was someone who loved me and supported me in a unique way. A tremendous loss and painful memory. Yet when I recall the memory, I also remember peace in the room. I felt the presence of angels.

Now, as I look back, I see Jesus was there holding me and comforting me as my mother was passing into the arms of the Lord. It helps me not to fear death, but to know that God is there when we need him most. Indeed, he is with us always to wipe every tear from our eyes.

> Revelation 21:4 "He will wipe every tear from their eyes, and there shall be no more death or mourning, wailing or pain, [for] the old order passed away."

A big part of our life is not about challenging situations, but about overcoming memories of the past that immobilize us. Since we are a new creation in Christ, we need to think and act differently in that identity. Everything is new and must be treated differently.

> Isaiah 65:17, "See, I am creating new heavens / and a new earth; / The former things shall not be remembered / nor come to mind."

Seeking peace is so important. Peace is a fruit of the holy Spirit as seen in Galatians 5. Yet when we let uncontrolled painful memories take over our thoughts, we often are far from peace. Our mind focuses on despair—"The past is happening again or even worse." The Lord desires to put these thoughts at the foot of the cross. He yearns for us to take on his mantle of peace.

> John 16:33 "I have told you this so that you may have peace in me. In the world you will have trouble, but take courage, I have conquered the world."

The process of healing memories takes seven steps.

First, ask God to reveal the memory to you. When you ask, he will give it to you. We know scripture tells us "Ask and we will receive." We know whatever we ask, we will obtain according to his will.

In most cases, we don't want to recall the memory. It is too painful. We "numb it out" by addictions to food, sex, pleasure, working, money, shopping, gambling and many more distractions. Life is easier, we think, by not dealing with the pain. Praying for courage is so important—courage to see the truth regarding the causes of our addictions.

The second step is putting Jesus in the scene of all painful memories. This step involves imagination. What is Jesus doing in the scene? Loving you, in whatever way you need. He might be embracing you or holding your hand; in every case, your eyes are fixed on his eyes.

Think of Peter walking on the waters of Galilee. As long as Peter looked at Jesus, he was fine. As soon as he looked at the waves, he began to sink into the sea and had to be rescued before drowning. When we "abide in him, he will abide in us." Jesus promised us again and again to trust in him. He will carry our burdens and supply our needs according to "his riches and glory."

The third step in healing memories is to receive the love of Jesus. An openness to Jesus' love may be hard for many of us. We don't feel lovable. We feel shame, dirty, unworthy; we don't think God can forgive what we have done. In other cases, we don't want to love Jesus because we want to cling to grudges or we feel we can't forgive those who have hurt us. In either case, our inability to love or receive the love of Jesus immobilizes us. Pray to be open to receive the love of Jesus.

The next step, the fourth, is to praise God and trust that Jesus will forever heal the memory. Often, believing a painful memory can be forgiven or removed is difficult. In many cases, doing so may be a process, not completed in one session of prayer, but rather over a period of time. When we keep praising God as the God who heals our memories, as our redeemer and savior, little by little, the memory is removed from our thoughts.

Reconciliation is the fifth step in healing memories. Why is reconciling so important? In many cases, we need to forgive the other party or ourselves. I recall, while waiting in line to see the priest, asking the Lord for guidance regarding what to confess. The answer surprised me. Unexpectedly, it wasn't the usual sins and weaknesses. Jesus told me my biggest sin was not trusting him. Not trusting him? You see, when we don't trust Jesus, we are attempting to be God. We think we know best.

Reconciliation heals us by restoring us to unity with Christ. Sometimes, we need to receive the sacrament more than once a week. Whatever it takes to be healed. Look at it this way, it took many years to get where we are now; it often will take some time to be healed.

The sixth step is attending daily Mass. For many of us, daily Mass may seem too much to ask. We don't have time, don't get enough out of the liturgy, whatever excuse you use. The question is, how badly do you want to be healed of your memories and pain? Are you willing to do what will help you, even though it may be an inconvenient sacrifice?

When we say "Yes" to the Lord through his body and blood, we are well on the way to the healing of memories, as well as a general healing, which usually includes spiritually and physically.

The seventh and final step to heal painful memories is improving our prayer lives— practicing silent prayer and letting the Lord fill us with his love. Actually, try for an hour of prayer, possibly 20 minutes of simply listening to the Lord, 20 minutes of prayer and 20 minutes of whatever the Lord puts in your heart. Or perhaps we're moved to pray the Rosary or Divine Mercy Chaplet, read scripture or spiritual books.

Many of us would rather occupy our time with activities other than prayer. However, when we develop the habit of being with the Lord, it is no longer a chore but a delight. "Sitting" with the Lord fills us with the fruit of the holy Spirit. We become open to love and be loved, to receive his joy and to experience the peace that passes all human understanding. Too difficult? Try 30 minutes at first and then each day, add five minutes. God will give you the grace to pray in a way you had not thought possible.

Jesus died on the cross for our redemption. He also died on the cross for our pain and suffering, and to heal us spiritually, mentally, emotionally and physically. Jesus wants to heal every part of us—including our memories—so that we may have abundant life.

Jesus took on our suffering, our pain and our sins to make us whole. His wounds healed us!

> Isaiah 53 4-5, "Yet it was our pain that he bore, / our sufferings he endured. / We thought of Him as stricken, / struck down by God and afflicted, / but he was pierced for our sins, / crushed for our iniquity. / He bore the punishment that makes us whole, / by his wounds we were healed."

CHAPTER 11

LIVING THE JOY OF CHRIST

When we suffer trials and tribulations, we don't feel joyous. In fact, we experience anything but joy. We may be in panic mode or simply a state of trying to survive. It is interesting to me that the Bible includes more than 500 references to joy. 500! Maybe God is trying to tell us something?

There is a significant difference between joy and happiness. How many times have we said we just want "happiness" for ourselves, our family, friends and those we love? I strongly believe happiness is not truly the best for us. What should our heart's desire be? Joy!

Why joy? Because happiness is based on circumstance, and joy is based upon relationship. We are happy when our favorite teams win in sports. We also know there is a good chance they may lose the next time they play. We are happy over a salary raise until we see the taxes. Our emotions go up and down like a roller coaster.

With joy, we embrace a relationship with Jesus. Joy stands for "Jesus Over You." When we love Jesus we want to have a relationship with him. When we spend time with the Lord, he fills us with his presence, and we are filled with the joy no circumstance can change. This joy is the reason people who are imprisoned or being tortured can have incredible joy. Nothing can take that away.

Joy is a way of living. It is not a feeling, event or emotion. It is a state of being in love with Jesus. It is living and experiencing the greatest commandment given to us, "To love God with all our heart, soul, might and strength." To love with the love of God, with our whole being united with him. In the state of joy, we can say "Abba, Father" and mean it. God becomes a loving Daddy to us!

The state of joy almost compels us to receive the sacrament of Reconciliation often and to attend daily Mass. When we experience Mass, the scripture readings and liturgy prayers come alive. We truly participate in this heavenly banquet. Mass is not boring but alive with joy and love in a way we could scarcely conceive. We truly understand Nehemiah's proclamation.

> Nehemiah 8:10, "Rejoicing in the LORD is our strength."

With joy, we are less likely to experience sadness, unhappiness, depression or anxiety—anything that keeps us apart from Jesus. Joy and love become the foundation of evangelization and our service to the Lord. We want to share our joy with God's people.

Joy definitely leads to rejoicing! The word joy or rejoice is used 19 times in Paul's letter to the Philippians. In the fourth chapter, we are encouraged:

> Philippians 4:4-7 "Rejoice in the Lord always, I shall say it again, rejoice! Your kindness should be known to all. The Lord is near. Have no anxiety at all, but in everything by prayer and petition with thanksgiving, make your requests known to God. Then the peace of God that surpasses all understanding will guard your hearts and minds in Christ Jesus."

Many times, we don't feel like rejoicing because we aren't getting what we want in life. Perhaps our relationships are strained with our spouses, children, friends or co-workers. We might be struggling financially, physically or spiritually. We turn our eyes away from Jesus and begin to sink emotionally.

When and if that happens, it is important to repent and trust in Jesus. One way is to pray the Rosary, saying "Jesus, I Trust In You" with each of the 50 beads. Begin praising the name of Jesus as our rock, fortress and savior!

Let's look at the word "rejoice" more carefully and apply it to our lives.

The "R" stands for relationship. We must strive to be in right relationship with God, communicating with him as often as possible. We feel his gentle loving touch and listen to his messages. We surrender our lives to Jesus and love him with unconditional love.

In this relationship with God, our prayer life is different. Rather than a series of petitions, our prayers are those of praise and thanksgiving. We trust in him to supply our needs according to his glorious riches. We live the scripture passage from Thessalonians.

> 1 Thessalonians 5:16-18, "Rejoice always. Pray without ceasing. In all circumstances give thanks, for this is the will of God for you in Christ Jesus."

As joyful people, when we do encounter trials and adversity, we look at them differently. We let the words of the letter of James fill our hearts.

> James 1:2-4, "Consider it all joy, my brothers, when you encounter various trials, for you know the testing of your faith produces perseverance. And let perseverance be perfect, so that you may be perfect and complete."

The "E" in rejoice stands for evangelization. When we are joyous, we want to share the love and saving grace of Jesus with everyone we meet! We are called and respond to the call to spread the good news of Jesus Christ, as Mark's gospel recounts.

> Mark 16:15-18, "He said to them, 'Go into the whole world and proclaim the gospel to every creature. Whoever believes and is baptized will be saved; whoever does not believe will be condemned. These signs will accompany those who believe: in my name they will drive out demons, they will speak new languages.

> They will pick up serpents [with their hands], and if they drink any deadly thing, it will not harm them. They will lay hands on the sick, and they will recover.'"

With the joy of the Lord, we live the gifts and fruit of the holy Spirit. In my 40 years in the healing and evangelization ministry, the central ingredient for sharing Christ and healing is the love of Jesus, with joy of the Lord in my heart.

We receive joy when we share Christ with others. Our joy increases when we lay hands on the sick and see their joy as the Lord ministers to them, spiritually, emotionally and physically. Every day I share Jesus with others, I am filled with joy. Every day becomes a "great day" in the Lord!

The "J" stands for justice. When we have joy, we are moved to give back. Several years ago, I started an employment initiative. We meet weekly with those in transition and out of work, helping them with networking, resumes and interview skills. We try to connect them with other people who can hire them or help them find work. I also work closely with Saint Vincent de Paul to give food and help with shelter when necessary. For me, justice is using the gifts and skills God has given me to give to or share with others. These rewarding efforts allow me to focus on others and not my own issues and problems.

The "O" in rejoice stands for only. The one and only. I am reminded of the movie, "City Slickers." In the film, the character "Curley" holds up one finger and says that was the most important thing. What is our "one thing?" The answer "Jesus" is not a slam dunk. What is getting in our way in putting Jesus first?

A number of years ago, before I entered the Diaconate program, I travelled to France and visited the Church of the Miraculous Medal. At the communion rail as I was praying, I heard a voice say, "I will give you the gift of poverty." I was so shook-up, I ran trembling to the back of the church.

I now joke that I looked up to heaven and asked, "Can we talk about this?"

In reality, at that moment, I decided I would dedicate all my financial blessings to Jesus, as he directed.

When I got home, I discovered something else. The Beatitude, "Blessed are the poor in spirit for theirs is the kingdom of God" now meant something quite different to me. It meant the one thing I needed to do was to put God first above everything. Family, health, job, finances, you name it, everything. I developed severe back problems, got fired from my job, had our daughter stop speaking to us, lost a grandchild to stillbirth and much more. I thought I was living out the book of "Job 2."

God was breaking me down before I became a Deacon to put me back together and give me the grace to make him first in my life, ahead of all things. Eventually, God blessed me with a job, finances, restored family relationships and many graces.

The "I" stands for intercession. When we intercede for people we are acting in the name of Jesus, who stands at the right hand of the Father interceding for us.

Especially powerful is praying the rosary and interceding for another. Let God lead you to discover those for whom you should pray. When we talk to people who are struggling, pray for them immediately, just as you are speaking to them. God loves when we are his voice, mind, and heart, and we pray for others!

In the word rejoice, "C" stands for community. When we are in community with loving people who know Jesus, we have joy, strength and protection. We experience the love of Christ. Join some type of prayer

group, perhaps a small prayer-sharing or Divine Mercy group, a rosary gathering, an assembly with others, especially of the same sex—anything that puts you with other people who will support and strengthen your journey with the Lord.

The final "E" in rejoice stands for everlasting life. We know peace and joy when we understand we are destined to be with Jesus and our Father in heaven forever! As John states in the 14th chapter of his gospel, Jesus has built a mansion for us in heaven beyond anything we can imagine. Yes, we have trials and suffering here on earth. Let's keep our focus on Jesus. When we do, we remove the sting of the areas in our lives that weigh us down.

We all know life is difficult. When we strive for joy, our lives change for the better. Is it easy? We all know the answer to that. I believe if life was easy, without trials and tribulations, we wouldn't receive the "crown of life" when we die. We wouldn't hear the words of Jesus, "Well done my good and faithful servant."

My brother Bill and I have an exchange that goes like this: I ask him, "Why is life so hard?" He answers, "Because it is supposed to be."

Jesus was very clear that we would endure challenges and trials. He also was clear that he is greater than the world or any problem we face, and that we will never be burdened with more than we can handle. At times, that seems hard to believe. But it is true because we are told in scripture that it is true. I choose to believe it!

May the joy of the Lord fill your hearts and souls and that of your loved ones, now and forever!

Praise God! Now and Forever!

CHAPTER 12
EXPECT AND EXPERIENCE MIRACLES!

It is very hard for us to believe that God's miracles are always there for us. Think about how much you love those closest to you? Your spouse, children, close friends and people who mean so much to you? Is there anything you won't do for them?

A huge part of spiritual growth is expecting God to be God and to shower us with his blessings. When we are going through adversity, it is hard for us to see that with God, "All things work for good for those who are called and who love God."

Ironically, God allowed me to experience his miracles in the midst of adversity while writing this book. Part of our ministry, Spirit Filled Hearts, is working as missionaries, called to minister to God's people in distant lands.

Perhaps you have been called to do something your flesh fights. Not exactly what you want to do, but God has a purpose for you. Jesus doesn't ask us whether or not it "feels good" or it is the right timing. He simply says, "Follow me."

And that's exactly what happened. Our friend, Father Victor, an Augustinian priest, invited us to minister to the Augustinian Sisters of Divine Mercy and the people they serve in their hospitals, clinics, schools and churches in Indonesia.

We were in the middle of the jungle, much of the time in Indonesia, home to the largest Muslim population in the world. The Sisters asked if I minded praying over Muslims and Buddhists. Of course! I would love to pray for them! They are all God's people and loved by God passionately.

To say the trip was challenging is an understatement. We were gone for 15 days and in one demanding stretch in seven different locations over seven nights. Those of us from the West can be spoiled. I am not used to being without showers, running water or electricity. Brown water? Not exactly the Marriott!

Of course, there also were the heat, the rain, the bugs, especially the "Jurassic Park"-like mosquitoes. Foolish me. Usually mosquitoes do not bother me very much. Not here. I was like a pinball machine. Bites everywhere!

Someone said to me when I returned that I will only truly realize how many miracles occurred on this trip until I am in heaven. The people waited for hours upon hours to be prayed over. We saw lives changed in dramatic ways. In many ways, it started with the Sisters. A number of them said they had never experienced "healing prayer" and felt God's love to the degree that they experienced it.

We experienced a number of people in bondage to demonic influence. Potions, charms, New Age items. The manifestations were powerful, like my wife and me especially with the young. God's grace and miracles overcame them. In one case, a young girl was screaming and in great anguish over what the enemy was doing to her.

Her parents were with her when we ministered to her. I asked if they "were involved with the Occult in any way or New Age items?"

The father, to my disappointment, nodded his head. He explained to us that someone from South Korea had given him potions, stones, ointments, bracelets, etc. He was told they would give him and his family power and protection.

Lies of the enemy! What they gave them was bondage and slavery to evil. In particular, their daughter, whom they said they loved, was in great bondage.

It was apparent to me that we had to destroy the source of the demonic influence. We learned that they lived close to the church where we had Mass and the healing service. Much to my surprise, the Sisters insisted that we go to their house.

When we arrived, we discovered some very interesting things. The parents had not merely one or two of these demonic-based items. There were so many I was stunned. Bracelets, chains, potions, charms, etc. On and on and on. A big bag of materials that kept growing. We took the necklaces from the parents. The bracelets and everything else.

I kept saying, "What else? What else?" And guess what? They brought out more and more and more.

Evil needs to be removed totally. No compromise. The miracle? I will long remember the 14-year old daughter. The young girl—who had been in incredible bondage, screaming and in pain—was filled with the Holy Spirit, beaming with smiles and joy. She was totally and completely healed!

Was this a miracle? Well, let's go back to the definition, "God's supernatural intervention in our lives." Would this had happened if we didn't go to Indonesia? With God, all things are possible, but clearly our saying "Yes" without hesitation to going on this Mission opened the door to the miracle and healing!

So where does the adversity come into play here? It often can occur when we least expect it. After ministering to thousands of people, having people wait in line for hours upon hours, toward the end of the trip, several in our missionary team began to experience symptoms of chills, fever and lethargy.

I, too, started to get chills, fever and weakness. I didn't think much of it because I was still on a "high" from God's grace and healing. Each day I got weaker. It became more difficult to function.

The team finally returned home and one of the people from Jakarta sent me a note. He had been positively diagnosed with Dengue Virus Fever. What? What is that? Coming from the West, I had never heard of this disease, transmitted by infected mosquitos.

Sure enough, when I arrived home I was tested for Influenza, which was negative. Dengue? My doctor had never seen a case. The medical lab took five days to report the result. Positive!

Unbelievable! In a million years, I never expected this level of adversity. This level of weakness and sickness is hard to fathom if you have never experienced it.

But the challenge became even more intense. I had just ministered to thousands and had suffered from the conditions and the intensity of the trip. My reward? Dengue Virus Fever?

Maybe this is what you have felt or currently feel in the middle of a trial?

We must again recall that "God's ways are not our ways." My brothers and sisters, it is essential that we learn an extremely important lesson. Ready? We are not God! Don't try to be. Don't try to figure it out.

We immediately seek the meaning of an adversity. Maybe we should go to an ant and ask the question, "what does it mean?" Our ability to understand is at the same level as the lowly ant.

We cannot see the future or determine why trials and adversity happen. What we can ascertain is we are loved, this is not heaven, and God is blessing us no matter what has occurred.

As I write this, I am experiencing miracles in a way that I had not experienced before. The trip is over, but the sickness continues. God is showering me with people praying for me, loving me and giving me blessings.

When we face adversity, look for miracles even more diligently. When things don't go our way, expect God to act in an even more powerful way.

Don't give up, but praise God for everything he is doing in your life, and you will experience even more divine intervention, called miracles.

CHAPTER 13

TRANSFORMATION THROUGH PRAISE

Praise changes everything! One of my most popular CDs is the title of this chapter. We are transformed in every way when we learn how to praise God.

It starts with the reality of the question, "What is praise?" For most of us, we think praise is being thankful. It is not! Being thankful is a byproduct of praise, but it is not praise.

Praise describes the "attributes of God," acknowledging God for who he is: The Lord of Lords, the Alpha and Omega, the Prince of Peace, our Savior, our Redeemer, our Shield, our Protector, our Comforter, Love, Our Advocate, the God of Mercy, our Rock, Creator, the Word Made Flesh, and on and on. Review the Catholic Litany of Praises.

The word Praise appears 550 times in scripture. Read chapter 150 of Psalms as a reflection of the importance of praise.

Psalm 150 reflects importance of praise:

> Psalm 150:6 "Let everything that has breath / give praise to the LORD."

Everything? Everything! We give glory to God when we praise him. Psalm 22 tells us that God inhabits the praises of his people.

How important is praise? Everything coming out of our mouth should involve praise in some way.

> Hebrews 13: 15-16 "Through him let us continually offer God a sacrifice of praise that is the fruit of lips that confess his name."

How is this possible? We see the answer to this in the Old Testament book of the prophet Isaiah

> Isaiah 43:21 "The people whom I formed for myself that they might announce my praise."

My brothers and sisters, we were created to praise God in everything we think, say and do. All of creation was created to praise God.

> Romans 8:22, "All creation is groaning in labor pains even until now."

In Luke's gospel, Jesus was asked to stop his disciples from praising God; his answer:

> Luke 19:40, "if they keep silent, the stones will cry out!" We are told to pray without ceasing in scripture, but I believe we are to

praise without ceasing.

When we truly learn how to praise, everything changes. Our life will never be the same. We are told to give thanks in all circumstances in 1 Thessalonians, but I believe we praise God in all circumstances for what he is doing in our lives. Dengue fever? Praise him for what we receive as a result of the illness.

People can disagree, but I feel it is highly unlikely, even impossible, to be anxious, depressed, discouraged or any other negative emotion when we are praising God. Think of Peter walking on the water. Eyes on Jesus, great miracles. Eyes off Jesus, he sinks.

When we praise God, we are transformed into his image. We truly become his ambassadors. A byproduct of praising is receiving the peace of Christ. We grow in the love of Jesus until our lives becomes reflections of that love.

When trials and adversity come, we should kick praise into "high gear." Make it the focus of our life, the core of our being.

Let's reflect on the word "praise" to help us implement it in our lives.

The "P" stands for presence. In the Garden, Adam and Eve were in the presence of God. When they sinned, they hid and soon were banished from God's presence. We seek the presence of God in everything we think, say, and do. Certainly, with the Mass and the sacraments, prayer and adoration we experience God's presence in a special way.

In the Lord's prayer, we praise the Father, "Hallowed by thy name." When we praise God, we put ourselves in his presence.

How do we do that throughout the day? When we wake up, begin praising God for being the God of creation, our provider, and our protection. Let praise fill our hearts and souls.

When we eat breakfast, praise him for being the God who grants our needs according to his riches and glory. Attend the great sacrifice of praise—the Mass—to start the day in the right direction.

When you are driving to work or school listen to praise music, and praise him with all your heart. At stop signals or lights, praise him for being his son or daughter.

During the day, use the opportunity to praise God before or during meetings, phone calls or conversations.

Read the Psalms during the day, especially those regarding praising God. Give thanks and praise for everything happening to you.

If possible, make time for adoration. Praising God for his Eucharist and presence.

Praise him by praying "in the spirit." Praying in tongues is God within you praising God the Father in a language you don't understand.

If possible, find time to praise God by instrument, music or song of some kind. It pleases God when we praise him in this way!

When we sleep, we can learn how to praise God in our dreams. We often are attacked by the enemy through dreams. Discover how to praise God when you are under attack to defeat the slings and arrows of the enemy.

The "R" in praise stands for restoration. Do you have a relationship that needs to be restored? Begin praising God for that person, blessing them by your love and prayers.

Many of us had or have bosses who drive us crazy. Instead of asking God to change or remove them, begin praising God for giving you the exact boss you need for your spiritual growth!

This situation happened to me several times. Particular people in my career were huge problems. With them, whatever I did seemed to be wrong. When I began to praise God for them, not only did my attitude change, but the way I was treated changed dramatically. I sincerely praised God for them and wanted what was best for them. In every case, each of them became friends and major supporters of me and what I was doing.

Try this also with those closest to you. A spouse or child. At one point, I looked at my daughter and asked why she wasn't respectful like other daughters. We had years of conflict.

When my attitude changed and God revealed to me that I had the exact daughter I needed for me and I for her, everything changed. I began to praise God for my daughter exactly the way she was. Wow! God blessed the relationship in a huge way! Trust God and try it with your heart! Praising God for people closest to you changes everything!

The "A" in praise stands for attitude. Think of about how you pray. Are most of your prayers petitions in which you want God to change something? I often joke that the number-one prayer God hears is, "Lord, change my spouse." The number-two prayer is, "Lord, change my children."

We think we know best, but when we realize we are not God, and we allow God to transform our attitude, everything changes around us. We are joyful because we accept what God plans for us and our lives. We don't harbor expectations that lead to disappointment. We embrace Romans 8:28, that all things work for good for those who love God and are called according to his purpose.

An attitude of praise protects us against the evil one, gives us solid mental health and even will make a big difference with our physical wellbeing.

The "I" in praise stands for intercession. In Psalms, we read:

> Psalm 100:4-5, we read "enter his gates with thanksgiving, / his courts with praise. / Give thanks to him, bless his name."

Do you want miracle after miracle to happen in your life? Learn how to praise and expect miracles in the midst of adversity.

I grew up in Glendale, California. Fires were common in the hills surrounding my parent's house. When the "Santa Ana" winds began to blow, the fire danger was often acute.

One particular year, it was particularly horrible. The winds were gusting 60-80 miles per hour, and the flames were awful. A number of homes in my parent's neighborhood had already burned down.

I stood on the lawn with a little garden hose, feeling helpless. Suddenly, God revealed to me the importance of praising him for being the God of the wind, fire, protection and everything. To praise and trust him in all things.

It was 7 p.m., and I begin to praise him for being the God who calmed storms, like those on the Sea of Galilee. The fire fighters came by to urge us to leave immediately for our safety. They said they had no control over the fire. We left and went to another location.

The next morning, I returned very early to see if the house was still standing. To my surprise, there was no fire damage, and no additional houses had burned down.

I called over a fire fighter. He looked at me and his eyes widened as he said, "Last night at 7 p.m., the wind shifted. No one expected or predicted it, and the fire burnt itself out with no additional damage to any homes."

Wow! Praise God! Exactly the time I was praising God for being the God of protection and creation!

I could go on and on with many examples of the results of praising God in adversity, but I will share just one more. I love to use scripture as a foundation for God's miracles when things are not going well. One example is the multiplication of loaves and fishes.

For many years, we had a team of 50-60 people who went to the hills of Tijuana in Mexico and built small homes with an organization called "Corazon."

One particular year, I was leading the paint team and noticed we had run out of paint before we were to paint the interior of the small home. We had been shorted paint supplies, and we used too much on the exterior. The only thing left was the goo lining the side and bottom of the paint cans. The team members asked me what to do.

I began praising God for being the God of multiplication. I praised fervently. Then I asked them to fill it with water and prayed over the paint can, praising God.

There were seven people painting that day. All of them dipped their brushes into the can of "paint." Wow! My eyes dilated when I saw the color of the paint was the same as the exterior color.

I began to praise God even more. Then whatever was in the can ran out. They asked me, "What do we do now?" I of course, praising God fervently, said, "Add water."

Much to my amazement, the paint color for the remainder of the room was the same color. Praise God! Now and forever!

The "S" in praise stands for strength. When you feel like giving up, praise God. Scripture encourages us.

> Nehemiah 8:10 "rejoicing in the LORD is your strength!"

> Psalm 28:7 "The LORD is my strength and my shield."

When we are discouraged, feeling like we want to give up, that is the time to praise even more.

What happened with the walls of Jericho? This city had never been defeated. Joshua 6 tells us the Israelites marched around the city walls seven times. On the seventh time, they praised God with shouts and instruments. What happened? The walls began to come down, and the city was defeated. Praising God brings miracles.

When Moses praised God in Exodus 17. the battle turned and they won. In 2 Chronicles 20, King Jehoshaphat appointed singers to praise the holiness of God at the front of his army. They began to praise God for his mercy and goodness and won a great battle!

Some of you are reading this book and struggling with major challenges. Spiritual, mental, relationship, financial or physical. No challenge is too big for God. Every challenge can be defeated when we learn how to praise him in all things!

The "E" in praise stands for expect miracles. When we praise God, everything changes. It is then God's grace is unleashed. I witnessed this one day at a conference

I attended during which I stood at the podium in front of 7,000 people and called out healing of macular degeneration in three parts of the arena. The next day three women reported being instantly healed! It was because of the praise and the mercy of Jesus!

When we praise God, we are in his presence. When we praise God, our relationships are restored. Try praising God in your prayer rather than reciting a nonstop petition. I often tell people to praise God when praying the rosary and see how it changes God's grace. Intercede for others by praising God rather than just say prayers of petition. Understand that praise is our strength at all times. Finally, after 40 years of ministry, I know that when we praise God and expect miracles, incredible things happen. Not necessarily when we expect them or how we expect them, but better than we can ever imagine.

It can feel counter-intuitive to praise God in the midst of trials and adversity. Yet that is exactly what we are to do. Jesus, I Trust In You!

CHAPTER 14

THE POWER OF LIVING A SACRAMENTAL LIFE

I am totally convinced we need, as Catholics, to understand the power, importance and critical nature of living a Sacramental Life.

The Roman Catholic Church teaches in the *Catechism of the Catholic Church* that the sacraments, on page 898, are "An efficacious sign of grace instituted by Christ and entrusted to the Church, by which divine life is dispensed to us through the work of the Holy Spirit." (774, 1131). The visible rites by which the sacraments are celebrated signify and make present the graces proper to each sacrament.

Though not every individual receives every sacrament, the Church affirms that, for believers as a whole, the sacraments are necessary as the modes of grace divinely instituted by Christ himself. The Catholic Church is the sole dispenser of Christ's sacraments and is considered to be the universal "sacrament of salvation."

In the Catechism, we learn the Church is centered on the Eucharistic sacrifice and the sacraments. The Roman Catholic Church administers seven sacraments: Baptism, Confirmation, Eucharist, Reconciliation, Anointing of the Sick, Holy Orders, and Matrimony.

During the time of my formation as a Deacon, my Spiritual Director focused on the critical nature of the sacraments. The Norbertine priest asked me often how serious I was about my faith. Did I truly want to grow in holiness?

We often come up with countless reasons why we don't have time for daily Mass. It is a hassle, we need our sleep, our work schedule, and on and on. The primary question I have for each of you reading this book is, "Who wants you to go to daily Mass and who doesn't?" The Lord wants to give us "our daily bread." To bless us abundantly with grace, strength and blessings. Who doesn't want us to go to daily Mass? Well, you know the answer. The enemy would do anything to convince us not to go to Mass and receive the Body and Blood of Jesus Christ.

Month after month, my Spiritual Director challenged my faith intention. I came up with excuses to justify my laziness. The reality is that receiving the Eucharist daily was not a priority. However, what often occurs happened to me. God brings us to our knees. Something happens in life, and frequent Mass attendance was no longer optional for me. I needed

God. I needed grace. I needed supernatural strength and wisdom, and I needed it now!

At the time, I was a Senior Director of Sales for the State of California for a pharmaceutical company. We had a product for high cholesterol, called an HMG, with severe competition from other companies. California was and is an extremely significant state in which Managed Care Companies dictate what products are prescribed.

One week, I received phone calls and letters from nearly every major Managed Care Company revealing my company's product was to be removed from their formulary. My Sales Management team went crazy: wailing and gnashing of teeth. They asked me if they should update their resumes. They were panicking and giving up.

When we face adversity, whether it be personal, health, relationships or financial, God gives us a way out. However, God wants us to change our behavior, trust him and turn our lives to him.

There was no way out of my business situation through my innate wisdom. However, I knew God had allowed this to happen, and he had a solution if I got close to him.

What was the solution? Daily Mass. No matter what. My busy schedule? It didn't matter. Getting close to Jesus is and will always be the solution.

I began attending daily Mass and realized it was impossible to be serious about holiness without it.

What happened with the business? Miracle after miracle. God give me an idea that led to doubling my business, getting promoted and becoming a hero to senior management. I am totally convinced these blessings would never have happened without daily Mass. Nothing I do will change its importance.

Another sacrament is critical to our spiritual growth and to overcome trials and adversity is Reconciliation. I find it tragic that people do not understand how essential Reconciliation is.

Most of us feel we don't need to receive this sacrament. We haven't done anything that bad, we are embarrassed, don't want to take the time to receive the sacrament or countless other reasons.

The truth is so different. How often do we sin? Any daily examination of conscience, however brief, we realize we sin throughout the day. These sins are a turning away from God in thoughts, words or actions. However, they also include sins of omission. When do we simply ignore the Lord when he wants us to minister to someone or do what he is whispering us to do? Do we desire to be in the will of the Lord? Do we truly seek him with all our heart, soul, might and strength?

Reconciliation gives us the grace to overcome trials that come from the enemy, the wisdom to turn to God in prayer, and the strength to avoid sin.

At times, I will receive reconciliation more than once a week. In fact, sometimes I attend daily. For most people, that seems radical. For me, if I am laboring under a severe trial, I am not trusting God as I need. Reconciliation gives me the strength to do the many things God is calling me to do.

For some reading this book, God may be calling you to Holy Orders. In the Catholic Church, it is a sacrament by which a man is made a bishop, priest or deacon and is dedicated to be an image of Christ.

I never expected to receive this sacrament and to become a deacon. God had a different plan. How do you know if God is calling you?

Turn to God. Ask and expect his answer to open or close the door only he can open or close. Some of you are now receiving a nudge from the Lord. Say "Yes" to it! Investigate religious life whether you are a man or woman. You won't regret it!

CHAPTER 15

CALLED TO EVANGELIZE

I love to administer the sacrament of Baptism for so many reasons. Welcoming the new person into the church! Letting the Holy Spirit wash clean original sin.

Perhaps my favorite part of the sacrament is the anointing with sacred chrism to be "priest, prophet and king." This oil is also used in confirmation. What does this mean? From the beginning, we are called to be evangelists!

I often like to point out three chapters in Scripture, Acts 1, Matthew 28 and Mark 16. The scene in each case is Jesus, ready to ascend into heaven. He is giving his disciples—and us—last-minute instructions. The most important things for us to do when Jesus is not with us.

When we go away on vacation or a trip, and we give instructions to someone to watch over our place, animals, etc. we are very specific. Jesus is giving his final instructions and was very clear what he wanted us to do.

> Matthew 28:19 "Go, therefore, and make disciples of all nations, baptizing them in the name of the Father, and of the Son, and of the holy Spirit."

Good news! That is the Greek root of the meaning of the word evangelization. What is this good news? If we were to ask 100 Catholics to define the "good news" of Jesus Christ, what would we hear?

In my experience, most do not know or even remotely understand the enormity of what God has done for us. The well-known scripture verse from John's gospel is a good place to begin.

> John 3:16 "For God so loved the world that he gave his only Son so that everyone who believes in him might not perish but might have eternal life."

You have been chosen to deliver this message to the world, starting with those people God has put in your life: your family, spouse, children, grandchildren, friends, and co-workers, those you encounter in business, school, life situations, etc. Everyone!

When are we asked to deliver this "good news?" Paul is very clear to his letter to Timothy.

> 2 Timothy 4:2 "Proclaim the word; be persistent whether it is convenient or inconvenient; convince, reprimand,

encourage through all patience and teaching."

I love this verse because it says it all for me. We are not to focus on the right timing to share God's good news, but to do it early and often. We have been chosen.

> John 15:16, "It is not you who chose me, but I who chose you and appointed you to go and bear fruit that will remain, so that whatever you ask the Father in my name he may give you."

In Second Vatican Council documents, we are reminded that "evangelization is at the very heart of the church." Saint John Paul II told us, "I sense that the moment has come to commit all the church's energies to a new evangelization. No believer in Christ, no institution of the church, can avoid this supreme duty: to proclaim Christ to all peoples."

Pope Emeritus Benedict XVI called a Synod, a gathering of 250 Bishops from around the world, in October 2012 to declare the "Year of Faith" and better define the "New Evangelization."

He described his definition of this new evangelization. "Directed to the whole world, its many cultures and peoples, to those who have never of Christ and those who have heard the good news but forgotten what it means to follow Christ."

When we think of evangelization, we often picture ourselves in foreign lands—such as my recent trip to Indonesia. However, what the church wants us to understand is that evangelization means reaching out to those closest to us. Every minute of every day may bring an opportunity to bring the good news of Jesus Christ. Are you up to the challenge?

Saint Paul was very clear in respect to the importance of our responsibility in sharing the good news of Jesus Christ.

> Acts 20:26-27 "And so I solemnly declare to you this day that I am not responsible for the blood of any of you, for I did not shrink from proclaiming to you the entire plan of God."

I think about these verses all the time and the tremendous responsibility we have for each other. A responsibility made even more real to me in a dream.

In the dream, I saw Jesus calling to me in the middle of a beautiful green meadow. He called over to me, embraced me and said, "Well done, my good and faithful servant."

He then gestured to the horizon, and I saw many people walking to me. There were at first 50, then 100 and finally, literally thousands coming up to me and thanking me for telling them about the saving power of Jesus.

I remember saying to these people, "I don't know who you are." They explained that on a certain date, I proclaimed the good news of Jesus Christ at an event, and the person listening told another person, who told another person who told them. This ripple effect is exactly how it works!

I remember in the dream feeling great joy! However,

the dream contained a warning and a second part. A small group of people with their heads down walked up to me and said to me, "You knew the good news of Jesus Christ and choose not to say anything to me."

This part of the dream shook me to the core. I realized it is not doing people a favor by remaining silent. We are so concerned about "offending" people. The biggest offence is silence.

I understand I don't have the responsibility to "save" people. Only Jesus saves. My responsibility is to tell people about the saving power of Jesus Christ.

Saint Paul is very clear what we are to do.

> Romans 10: 14-15,17 "But how can they call on him in whom they have not believed? And how can they believe in him of whom they have not heard? And how can they hear without someone to preach? And how can people preach unless they are sent. As it is written, 'How beautiful are the feet of those who bring [the] good news!' Thus, faith comes from what is heard, and what is heard comes through the word of Christ."

We have not been left orphans. We have been given the power of the Risen Christ and the holy Spirit.

> 1 Corinthians 4:20 "The kingdom of God is not a matter of talk but of power."

How do we get this power? By wanting it, asking for it and expecting to receive it.

> Luke 11:9. "Ask and you will receive; seek and you will find; knock and the door will be opened to you."

Jesus told his disciples and us clearly, we will receive the power of the Holy Spirit.

> Acts 1:8 "But you will receive power when the Holy Spirit comes upon you and you will be my witnesses in Jerusalem, throughout Judea and Samaria, and to the ends of the earth."

Great miracles of evangelization will occur when we expect the power of the Holy Spirit will work through us. We see great growth in the Catholic Church where the gifts of the Holy Spirit are flowing freely. In Brazil, there are 127 million Catholics. In Africa, the gifts are common and places such as the Congo, Nigeria, Uganda are exploding! In the last 100 years, the Catholic population has grown from 1% of the region's population to 21%. In fact, Africa is now providing vocations to many places in the world.

Our purpose in life is to make a difference. To build up the body of Christ. We remember the Baltimore Catechism in which we are told we are to love God, know God and serve God. Many of you are thinking you are too busy, aren't qualified or don't know what to say. The next chapter of the book will give you a step-by-step process of being the light of Christ.

All of my challenges and problems melt away when I am sharing the love of Jesus with other people. It is not about us. It is about Jesus and sharing his infinite and unconditional love and salvation!

CHAPTER 16

BECOMING THE LIGHT OF THE WORLD

We get depressed or down because of our circumstances. We don't experience the miracles God wants to give us because of our lack of faith and inappropriate focus.

I am 100-percent convinced when we are in trial, and when we share the love of Jesus, everything changes. We feel joy; the anxiety of our challenges seems so much less severe. God transforms us into his image. We depict the fruit of the Spirit and have more love, joy, peace, patience, kindness and everything else worthy of God's grace.

Jesus was extremely clear. We must be the light of the world. Again, and again, God has given me the commandment to take back the darkness. The darkness of sin, addiction, slavery to the world, flesh and the enemy.

Matthew 5: 14-16 "You are the light of the world. A city set on a mountain cannot be hidden. Nor do they light a lamp and then put it under a bushel basket; it is set on a lampstand, where it gives light to all in the house. Just so, your light must shine before others, that they may see your good deeds and glorify your heavenly Father."

It is critical for us to learn how to share our faith. God wants us to just that, and yet, we often are afraid. We feel inadequate and ill-prepared, and avoid it like the plague.

There are seven steps to help you be "the light of the world." The first is the desire to share your faith. This seems obvious, but most of us don't get past the first step. If we seek, we will find. If we desire God's will, it will be given to us.

In my experience, sharing our faith and the love of Jesus transforms our attitude and mood in all circumstances. Are we open to at least trying?

One day I got a flat tire on my car. "What?" I was grumbling and complaining. My plan was not happening. I was sitting on a bench waiting for my car to be repaired when the Lord came upon me with a message. I felt him telling me the reason for my flat tire was to tell the garage manager to return to God and that God loved him.

I got up from the bench and went to find the garage manager. When I found him, I introduced myself as the local Deacon and asked him if he was Catholic.

Much to my surprise, he said, "Yes."

I thought I was out of the woods until he added to his comment, "But I haven't been to church in 30 years."

Okie Dokie! I told him I had been sitting on the bench, patiently waiting, when I felt God telling me a message to share with him. I shared the message for the man to return to God. His eyes widened, and he told me he had had several dreams the past week in which God appeared to him to return to the Mass and church with his wife and family. He committed to me that he was going to do just that!

The second step in becoming a light to the world is to enhance your relationship with Jesus. Do you know Jesus in your heart? Do you communicate throughout the day in a two-way exchange?

So many people say they never hear from God. One of my favorite stories is the one of Saint Joan of Arc, before the Queen of France who asks her, "How can a peasant girl hears from God and the Queen of France does not?" Joan answered quickly, "Your highness, God is communicating to you all day long, but you are not listening."

To be in relationship, we must know each other. God has not left us orphans. He promised us he would guide us to all truth. We must expect him to talk to us in the stillness of prayer, through scripture, other people, songs, quiet whispers to us and many other ways. The more we are open to God's voice, the more we will hear him.

Participation in Mass, praying the rosary, adoration,

reading scripture and having an hour alone with the Lord are things that draw us closer to Jesus and allow us to hear him more clearly.

The third step in sharing our faith is to become the personification of the love of Jesus. I love what Saint Peter says about loving one another.

> 1 Peter 1:22b "love one another intensely from a [pure] heart."
>
> 1 Peter 4:8 "Above all, let your love for one another be intense, because love covers a multitude of sins."

How do we love God and each other intensely? By sharing our faith with people. By letting people know how much God loves them and that, as written in the 8th chapter of Romans, nothing will separate them from the love of God.

I remember when my brother was going through a hard time and didn't have a relationship with God. I prayed the love of Jesus into him and told him I was more convinced God was real than the table in front of us was real.

You are the fifth gospel! Tell people your story in love. This is not about how much scripture you know, Theology, being an expert in Catholicism, but it is about loving people with the love of Jesus.

For many years, we prayed with another couple on Friday night after going out to dinner. One particular night, we had been praying for four hours. It was 11:30 p.m. God had me and us praying over a woman who had childhood stress and needed emotional healing. I prayed for the love of Jesus to flow through me into her and to heal her of her wounds and memories.

Suddenly, with a tremendous burst of the love of Jesus flowing through me into her, I saw the Blessed Mother standing a few feet away, praying with us. In a sequence of a few seconds, I saw her praying, her cloak, twelve stairs over her head, angels at her feet and then the entire room filled with angels. I am convinced the Blessed Mother is always there, as a Spiritual Mother, praying with us with her special love and the love of Jesus!

The fourth step is obedience. We know we are tell others about Jesus, whether we feel like it or not. I had an unique experience when I was on the East Coast flying from Manchester, New Hampshire, to Philadelphia. I was sitting on the plane in a window seat with the middle seat empty.

I was reading the Bible and it was 7:30 p.m. I was tired and didn't want to talk to anyone. The Lord came upon me and told me to talk to the woman in the aisle seat.

I definitely was not embracing the obedience rule because I told the Lord I was tired and didn't want to do it. Every few minutes, I felt the Lord, on a 45-minute flight, tell me to talk to her. I keep refusing. Then about 20 minutes into the flight I sneezed, and the woman said "God bless you."

I felt as if a bell went off. I smiled, then asked the woman if she was going home to see her family? She answered, "Yes, I am going home to see my husband and daughter. They think I was at a work conference, but I was with my lover."

Wow! Are you kidding me? All within the first few seconds! She even pulled out a *New Yorker* magazine about a woman cheating on her husband. She said she was a Christian, like me, but no one is perfect.

I looked into the air and prayed. God came to me with a question. I asked her, "Do you ever pray with your boyfriend?" She looked at me and said that she prayed with her husband but had not prayed with her boyfriend.

I then said, in love, does her relationship with her boyfriend bring her closer to God? She looked at me, with tears in her eyes, and she said the moment was so much of what God does, "God doesn't come to you with a brick but with a feather, and you are my feather. She promised to leave her boyfriend and to return to God.

The fifth step is to embrace the power of the Holy Spirit. When we pray for healing we show the love of Jesus in a way pleasing to him. Miracle after miracle occurs when we simply say "Yes" to his love. Many times when the power of the Lord flows and people feel the love of God, they are healed spiritually, mentally and physically.

The sixth point is to "bloom where you are planted." You needn't go looking for people to share your faith with, they will come to you.

I was working in the "field" with a sales rep when she

asked me to pray over her. She had broken her wrist, knew I was a Deacon and in the healing ministry, and was sacred. When began that day, the last thing I felt I was going to do was share the love and healing power of Jesus with this particular sales rep.

She told me she was scared because she played tennis, and her wrist might never be the same again. I was in work mode and not Deacon mode when it became apparent the reason I was with her was to enhance her faith and have the healing of power of Jesus come to her.

I asked her to pull the car over and began to pray fervently over her to be completely healed. I asked her to turn to God completely and gave her a rosary from the Holy Land. She began to get emotional, feeling the love of Jesus.

A few months later, we were at a national meeting and she saw me. I was Vice President of Sales. She came running up to me extremely excited and jumped into my arms. I quickly asked her what had happened.

She told me an amazing story. She said she had gone to see the orthopedic surgeon who took off her cast and x-rayed her wrist's broken bone. After getting the x-ray results, the doctor came into the room astonished. His comment was, "I don't know what happened, but the x-ray didn't even show that you had ever had a broken wrist." It was completely healed!

The power of God is one of the most convincing things that can ever happen to us. We see his love, and it changes our lives!

The final step is to be a person of invitation. Most people respond to other people who are truly interested in whom they are as a person. How can we get to know them? When was the last time you invited someone to coffee, Mass, a meeting at church, a social function, or something at your house? A great way of evangelization is small group meetings. Our parish has implemented the Renew International Program called "Be My Witness." The program's small groups focus on topics relating to evangelization.

The early church developed by gathering daily and growing as a community. It can't happen without that.

> Acts 2: 46-47 "Every day they devoted themselves to meeting together in the temple area and to breaking bread in their homes. They ate their meals with exultation and sincerity of heart, praising God and enjoying favor with all the people. And every day the Lord added to their number those who were being saved."

My brothers and sisters, I know it is hard. Life is difficult. That is why, when we persevere, we have the opportunity of receiving the "crown of life."

When we focus on sharing our faith, everything changes. Our attitude becomes one of hope and belief. We trust God, and the miracles start flowing. Praise God! Now and forever!

CHAPTER 17

ANSWERING THE CALL

Picture yourself fishing on the shore of the Sea of Galilee. You've had a difficult day. Very few fish caught. You think and do things inconsistent with following God and being the devout person you desire to be. You mumble and complain, feeling sorry for yourself.

Suddenly, a stranger walks up to you. You feel incredible love emulating from this person. You see it in his eyes. He looks right through you with warm, glistening eyes and smiles. He speaks, "Come follow me!"

All you think is, "How is this possible?" Even if I wanted to, I have a family, responsibilities. I don't know this person. Where is the logic in following him?

While this scenario is more dramatic than most of us would ever encounter, at some level and in some way,

Jesus is calling you right now to follow him without reservation.

What about my problems? My financial responsibilities? My family? How is it possible?

This is my question to you, "Do you choose your problems and challenges or do you choose Jesus?" When we say "Yes" to the call of Jesus, we are like the Blessed Mother in her great assent, "Let it be done to me according to your word." We don't understand but know we don't have to understand. All we need is be obedient.

When we say "Yes" to Jesus, our world changes. We may expect our problems to disappear away immediately. That usually doesn't happen, but our attitude toward them changes. We don't give them the power we had previously.

So many people are trapped by the desire for a divine plan to be rolled out immediately. We want to know all is going to work and a step-by-step road map. It doesn't work that way because we must learn faith and trust. As Hebrews tells us, it is impossible to please God without faith.

Our focus needs to be one step at a time.

> Psalm 119:105, "Your word is a lamp for my feet, / a light for my path."

At the times of David and Jesus, lamps were tied to people's feet at night, which would project a few yards of light, but impossible to see much beyond that distance. Trust that God will lead you in the darkness.

I had an interesting dream in which I was driving a car filled with people. I was at the top of a major hill and had to choose one of two roads to proceed. The first was at the center of the hill. It looked like the best decision. At the hill's midpoint, the road was wide and straight. However, I couldn't see very far past where the road started due to fog and clouds.

Something made me not trust that choice. Even though it looked safe and the obvious choice. I decided to get out of the car before we started the trek down the hill. I stood on the edge of the hill, and there was a break in the fog. The road only went a short distant then plunged and ended. We would of gone into the ocean and certain death. It looked simple, but it was anything but easy.

I shuddered and went to the other road. It was not wide, but narrow, and very winding with hairpin curves. As I reached the road's beginning, before going down the hill, a man got out of the car and starting leading me, walking ahead of me, directing every part of the drive. I felt safe. It was Jesus with a big smile on his face.

Life is about making a decision on who will or what lead you. Will it be yourself, thinking you know best, taking the road that looks the easiest but really is a disaster? Or is it letting Jesus guide us because we know we can't do it?

We can choose to focus on our problems and only let Jesus in when everything is perfect, which will never happen. Or we can realize that we will always have issues and choose Jesus to lead us.

Okay, we make the right decision and choose Jesus. Now what? We pray and let him lead us. Don't try to figure it out. Go at God's speed. It might be slow or it might not be.

The first step is pray fervently and expect an answer. The Lord will reveal himself to you in a mighty way. The Holy Spirit will lead you to all truth. He will take you by the hand and lead you to Jesus and the Blessed Mother.

> John 14:6 "The advocate, the holy Spirit that the Father will send in my name; he will teach you everything and remind you of all that I told you."

The second step is to say yes to your passion. God will never give you an area completely foreign to where he has previously led you. It might be something someone had suggested to you. It might be an area you always wanted to do but didn't have the time, ability or courage to take action.

Often circumstances will open the door to change and a new direction to which God is calling you. A number of years ago, a woman in her fifties came up to me and said something had happened that dramatically impacted her life. She was fired from her job.

She explained that she had been working for more than 30 years and had never been unemployed. She admitted she didn't have a clue on what to do about finding a job—everything from writing a resume, interview skills, finding the right company, etc.

She then said something very powerful, "I know

others are like me and I want to help build a ministry to help those like me who are older and don't know where to start and what to do."

Awesome! With her as a catalyst the lives of hundreds were changed. The woman helped us organize the ministry logistically. We found people with human resource experience, leaders who knew how to coach people, technical people who helped with "Linked-In" and other social media opportunities, and many others volunteers.

As a result of this woman's "Yes," many hundreds of people have been hired and even more have enhanced their personal skills.

God will use whatever skills and experience we have, as displayed as the parable of the talents seen in Matthew 25. How do you know what to do? All you need is to say "Yes" to Jesus, and it will happen gently. Remember it is Jesus who will never break a "bruised reed."

We can do many things to build the kingdom. Hospitality, bereavement, visiting the sick, employment, young families, teaching religious education, social justice, prayer groups, lectors, Eucharistic minister, working with the homeless and countless other possibilities. You say "Yes" to Jesus, and he will do the rest!

Life is meant to be exciting and abundant. It always is when we are aligned with Jesus and doing his will for our lives. Do not worry. Do not be afraid. When we give our time, talents and treasures, God showers us with blessings!

> 2 Corinthians 9: 6-7 "Consider this: whoever sows sparingly will also reap sparingly without sadness or compulsion for God loves a cheerful giver."

I have found when the Holy Spirit guides us to minister to God's people, we receive the fruit of the Spirit that teaches us how to love passionately.

Let's look to the book of Samuel.

> 1 Samuel 3:10, "The LORD came and stood there, calling out as before: Samuel, Samuel! Samuel answered, 'Speak Lord, your servant is listening.'"

God is speaking to you right now. Calling you to an abundant life. Calling you to love passionately and receive God's passionate love. Say yes to his calling. You will never regret it!

CHAPTER 18

CALLED TO BE HOLY

My brothers and sisters, you were called to read this book. You are called to have a radical new life of wonder and joy. You are called to be holy.

We see this call to a joyful life in the Old Testament.

> Leviticus 20:26, "Therefore, you shall be holy; for I, the LORD, am holy, and I have set you apart from other peoples to be my own."
>
> Leviticus 11:44 "We need to make and keep ourselves holy because I am holy."
>
> 1 Peter 1:16, we are reminded to be holy because the Lord is holy.

When I ask people if they are holy, almost 100% of them say they are not, and most will even say they don't know anyone who is holy.

The reality? We are holy because we are called to be

holy and because of what Jesus has done for us by his death on the cross and his resurrection. He has wiped clean our sins and made us "whiter than snow." We must just say "Yes" to being holy.

We have been chosen to be holy.

> Ephesians 1:4 "As he chose us in him, before the foundation of the world, to be holy and without blemish before him."

How do become holy? There is a seven-step process that leads us to holiness.

The first step is to desire holiness. We are called to be holy. We are called to be Saints. Saint Mother Teresa told us we most desire to be holy and expect that we will receive it. What is more important to you than becoming holy? Nothing should be!

The second step is to surrender our life to Jesus. We can't get there if we have one foot in the world and one foot with Jesus. If we are lukewarm, Jesus will "spit" us out of his mouth as seen in Revelation 3. When we seek God with all our hearts, hunger and thirst for him, we will receive the grace for holiness.

The third step is to repent of our weakness and sins on an ongoing basis. Have we forgiven ourselves for our sins? Have we forgiven others for the hurt they have caused us? Let's get in the habit of examining our conscience at the end of each day and go to frequent Reconciliation.

The fourth step is to ask for faith. Faith that moves mountains and leads us to deeper holiness. Through faith we experience miracles. Faith, through the love of Jesus, heals us.

We have learned in this book that to receive more faith, we must ask for it. We must expect to "move mountains." What are you afraid of? It's okay that you don't "feel" faithful; ask and you will get it in abundance!

The fifth step is to learn how to pray fervently. Most of us pray by asking God for things. It is critical we learn how to pray from our hearts, beginning with praising God for who he is. Prayer and praise lead us to be thankful for what God has done for us. It often involves praying in the Spirit.

To what extent do we go to Adoration? It is amazing what a difference it can in our lives. I am on the Evangelization committee in my Diocese, and at one meeting the connection between fervent attending of Adoration and vocations was pointed out.

When we are one with God, "Abide in me and I will abide in you," we have the power, love and grace of our Father in heaven. We are connected with God through prayer, praise and the sacraments; we are doing his will. When we do the will of God, we live in holiness.

This also leads us to the Blessed Mother and the rosary. Praying through Mary is the best way to become a Saint. She guides us to the will of her son Jesus.

The sixth step toward holiness is to love fervently. Ask God to teach you how to love. It is the most important act you can perform. It starts with God teaching you how to open your heart to receive the love God has for you.

To love in holiness and with the love of the Father, we must learn how to forgive—a huge stumbling block for many. They try to come up with excuse after excuse on why they can't forgive.

My brothers and sisters, we have no choice if we want to be holy. Lack of forgiveness will prevent our "being set apart" or holy. Is holding on to anger, hurts, ill feelings worth it? The answer is no, especially considering what God has told us: we will be forgiven in the same measure we forgive others. That when we judge, we place that same judgement on ourselves.

Learn to love unconditionally by asking for it, repenting when you are not loving, and asking for the grace to receive how to love with the love of Jesus. Do not be prideful in your ability to love, since all love is of God and comes from God.

Finally, to be holy means you are living a sacramental life. It requires leading a life in which you hunger and thirst for the Mass and Eucharist. To what extent is your day based upon receiving the Eucharist or routinely going to Reconciliation?

When God has called us to be holy, he has called us to himself. He wants to give us every spiritual gift and blessing in the heavens.

The purpose of this book is to teach us that God is close to us at all times and especially when we face adversity and trials. No matter what we are going through God's love, grace and forgiveness is greater than God's love, grace and forgiveness is greater holiness. You were created to be an instrument of God's love, joy and peace.

May God our Father bless each of you and your loved ones with his abundant love, through the intercession of the Blessed Mother, the power of the Holy Spirit, in the name of Jesus, amen!

All praise, glory and honor be his now and forever, amen.

Made in the USA
Columbia, SC
15 August 2018